THE HOME CRAFTSMAN'S

WOODWORKING

TRICKS

OF

THE

TRADE

The methods expert craftsmen use to turn out better work and save themselves time and effort . . . Joint making, fastening and gluing . . . Ways to hold and clamp work . . . Power-tool expedients . . . Short cuts and repairs . . . Woods, plywoods and their best uses . . . How to combat warpage and shrinkage

EDITED BY

Arthur Wakeling

Consulting Editor

The Home Craftsman Magazine

WILDSIDE PRESS

The HOME CRAFTSMAN series of manuals:

How to Build Modern Kitchen Cabinets
How to Build Your Own Workshop Equipmen
How to Operate Your Power Tools
Selected Wood Turning Projects
The Practical Workshop Guide
Cabinets, Bookcases and Wall Shelves
Construction of American Furniture Treasures
99 One Evening Projects
Earning Extra Money in Your Workshop
Home Woodwork Projects
Garden Furniture, Barbecues and Fences
Money-Saving Home Improvements

INTRODUCTION—If you have spent even a
short time watching experienced carpenters and cabinetmakers at work, you must have considerable admiration
for the ease, assurance and extreme accuracy with which
they perform seemingly difficult operations.

Part of their skill, like that of all professional workers, is
due to long practice and thorough discipline in taking
pains at every stage of the work. But there is something
else. They also know a great many tricks of the trade. They
have absorbed in one way or another the knowledge of
how to work with tools and wood—a knowledge that represents the accumulated discoveries of skillful craftsmen
through the centuries.

Naturally, if you can acquire this information yourself,
you will be able to work with much greater ease and skill.
More than that, you will gain a better insight into the
basic principles of woodworking and will be able to solve
new problems as they arise with the same ingenuity that
a professional constantly brings to his daily tasks.

This book has been prepared to explain as many tricks
of the trade as possible. These have been grouped more

or less arbitrarily under some general subjects such as woodworking joints, ways to fasten parts together, gluing and its problems, methods and short cuts with both hand and power tools, the technique of holding and clamping work, and the selection and uses of woods and plywoods.

Far more has been compressed into this little volume than you are likely to realize from a first reading. If you make the book your workbench companion, however, and refer to it frequently, you will absorb more and more information. Even some of the ideas which you will perhaps never have occasion to use will actually help your work, because you will have a better idea of how experts have solved difficult and unusual problems. You will thereby be encouraged to work out original solutions of your own.

It is taken for granted that you have had a manual-training course at school or are familiar with one or more of the many available manuals which explain common woodworking operations, or else have picked up in some way or another a basic knowledge of woodworking. This book makes no attempt to duplicate that information, but rather to give you an insight into helpful tricks of the trade which you might otherwise never learn.

The major part of this material was prepared by editors of the Home Craftsman Magazine—Harry J. Hobbs, Milton Gunerman and the undersigned. Thanks are due to Howard R. Berry, art director; Arthur Collani, staff furniture designer, and Alvaro A. Altomare, director of the magazine's experimental workshop.

Others who contributed ideas are: George F. Burnley, Hal Geihm, E. J. Hartel, Arthur Hoelzer, Dick Hutchinson, M. E. Hutto, Seth Harmon, the late Charles A. King, Harry J. Miller, G. C. McClure, M. A. McCreary, Benjamin Nielsen, T. B. Owens, H. Ben Perry, George O. Pommer, Jr., John J. Rea, Ray Rogers, E. H. Roberts, Frank Shore, Charles H. Sleeter, Bill Smith, Morris A. Stewart, A. J. Schmidt, Whitney K. Towers, H. C. Wells, and Shirell Wright.

ARTHUR WAKELING
Consulting Editor, The Home Craftsman Magazine

Table of Contents

PART 1

Joints — The Essence of Woodworking

WHEN gluing two or more boards together to form a wide piece of stock, it is important that the joining edges be perfectly straight. If one piece is placed in the vise and the joining piece rested on it, any inaccuracy in the joint will appear as a dark line. Holding the pieces, still in position, against the light will show up any open places still more clearly, although it is hardly necessary to do this in most cases.

A simple but good test is to slide one joining edge back and forth over the other. If the edges are true, there will be some friction in moving them—a feeling the experienced woodworker soon gets to recognize readily. On the other hand, if the edges are a trifle convex, the ends will be slightly open as shown much exaggerated in Fig. 1, so that contact is made mainly

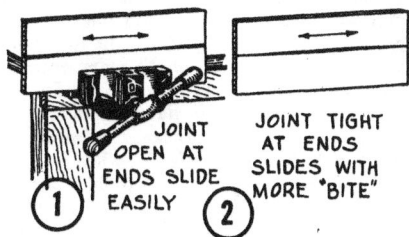

FACE SIDES PLACED TOGETHER

EDGES PLANED STRAIGHT, BUT NOT PERFECTLY SQUARE

ANGLES MATCH EXACTLY

JOINT OPEN AT ENDS SLIDE EASILY

JOINT TIGHT AT ENDS SLIDES WITH MORE "BITE"

in the middle section of the joint. Then one piece will slide over the other very easily. This is a bad indication, because a joint which is slightly open at the ends is much more likely to cause trouble than one which is tight at the ends although slightly open at the center as shown exaggerated in Fig. 2.

Whether or not the edges are square across does not worry a cabinetmaker so much. If the edges have been properly dressed on a jointer, they will, of course, be square. Machine jointing of stock for edge gluing will require that the jointer be correctly adjusted. The knives should be sharp and free of nicks. The finish cuts should be slight and the feed exceptionally slow to eliminate planer marks.

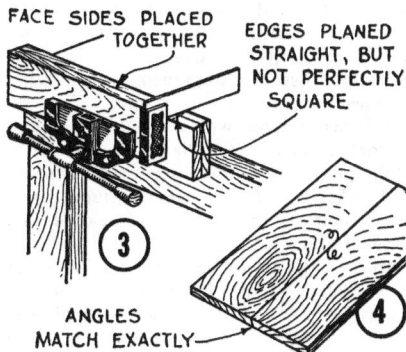

If the edges have been planed by hand, it does not matter particularly whether they are square or at a slight angle, provided the angles are alike but opposite to each other in direction so that one neutralizes the other, as it were. It is for this reason that two boards which are to be joined are sometimes placed in the vise together so that the joining edges can be planed in one operation, if the grain runs reasonably straight and doesn't have a tendency to tear up on one edge or the other.

In this case, the face sides of the boards are either placed together or on the outside so that the boards will open up like two pages of a book in order to bring the joining edges together. When this method is used, it is sufficient to be sure the edges are planed perfectly straight. They do not also have to be exactly square crosswise,

7

because the angles will be the same on both pieces as shown in Fig. 3 and will counteract each other when the pieces are in position for gluing as indicated in Fig. 4. The same principle holds true if the edges are planed separately.

A well-made joint, if properly glued with any high-quality wood glue, will be as strong or stronger than the wood itself and will last as long, especially if a modern, moisture-resisting glue is used. You may then ask, "Why are dowels so often used in this type of joint, or why are tongue-and-grooved or splined joints used?"

One reason is that boards that have been accurately bored for dowels or machined for tongue-and-grooved or splined joints are much easier to assemble because the parts are kept in alignment while being clamped.

Another reason, which has less validity, is that amateurs are likely to distrust a plain joint. They have seen old furniture and other woodwork where glued joints have come apart, but do not realize that these failures were due either to poor workmanship or to deterioration of older type glues which could not resist the strains set up by the cycles of high humidity in summer and extreme dryness in winter that occur in most modern homes. There is, of course, some justification for this mistrust on the part of those who will not take sufficient care to dress the joining edges properly and are not willing to take pains with the gluing and clamping operations. Furniture designers often indicate doweled joints in their plans as precautionary measure for this very reason.

It is obvious, therefore, that the home craftsman can save himself considerable time and trouble and also insure better results in his woodwork if he will take the time to master the art of making plain edge-to-edge joints with professional skill.

Easily Made Dowel Joints

MUCH attractive modern furniture is being made by amateurs from ¾" plywood or wide boards with plain butt joints. This is particularly true of those who live in apartments where it is impossible to use power tools and also those who have not yet equipped their shops with any machinery.

The great difficulty with ordinary butt joints, as every beginner quickly discovers, lies in assembling the parts square and true.

Even if a large array of clamps of various types and sizes is available—and that is not usually the case—it is far from easy to hold the parts without slipping after glue has been applied and while nails or screws are being driven to reinforce the joints. The upshot is that more time is wasted in assembly than is gained by reason of using the butt joints.

As a result, many amateurs, in the absence of a bench saw and other power tools, turn to dowel joints. These are used more to align the parts properly in the as-

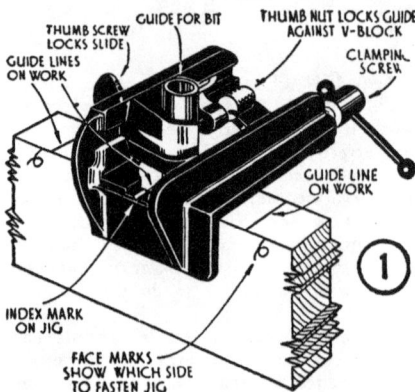

THUMB SCREW LOCKS SLIDE
GUIDE FOR BIT
THUMB NUT LOCKS GUIDE AGAINST V-BLOCK
GUIDE LINES ON WORK
CLAMPING SCREW
GUIDE LINE ON WORK
INDEX MARK ON JIG
FACE MARKS SHOW WHICH SIDE TO FASTEN JIG
①

sembly operation than for strength. Well-fitted and properly glued dowels are, however, very strong and are not likely to loosen if glued with any of the modern, durable glues.

Although the dowel joint ranks as one of the easiest to make, it does offer some difficulty to the beginner who has no drill press or other means of boring the holes accurately and has to do the work entirely with an ordinary brace and bit. In the first place, he finds it hard to locate the holes with sufficient accuracy so that the parts will line up perfectly when assembled. Second, he finds it troublesome to bore the holes perpendicular, which must be done for a good joint.

There are many solutions to both problems and once these are mastered, the dowel joint becomes simplicity itself to make. The time required is a little longer than that needed for a plain butt joint, but much if not all of that time is saved in the assembly; and, of course, the finished joint is stronger and more likely to stay tight permanently.

The first and best solution for the man who has to work entirely with hand tools is to use a commercial doweling jig, one

ONE TYPE OF
BIT DEPTH GAUGE

WOODEN SLEEVE
USED AS DEPTH GAUGE

To avoid having to measure and cut each dowel individually, it is best to bore all the holes to the same depth. The combined depth of the two matching holes should be about ⅛" greater than the length of the dowels to be used. To insure uniform depth, a depth gauge of some sort should be used on the bit as shown in Fig. 2. Note, however, that when this particular type of gauge is used with a doweling jig, it is placed upside down; that is, just the reverse of the way it is used when boring without the jig.

In the absence of a commercial depth gauge, a hole can be bored as straight as possible lengthwise through a square stick that is a little shorter than the bit itself. The stick is then planed true with the hole and the corners are rounded off roughly to make it less cumbersome, as in Fig. 3. This is cut to the desired length and slipped on the bit to serve like a regular depth gauge. When another job comes up and holes of a different depth are required, this wooden sleeve can be cut off to suit, provided it is long enough, or a second guide may be made in a few minutes. Several such guides will serve most of an amateur's needs nicely.

In the absence of a doweling jig, the woodworker is often advised to lay out the dowel-hole centers with try square, marking gauge and rule. This is good practice, but time consuming and not too easy for any but an experienced craftsman. The beginner had better disregard it. There are all sorts of ways to be sure the holes will line up without going to all that trou-

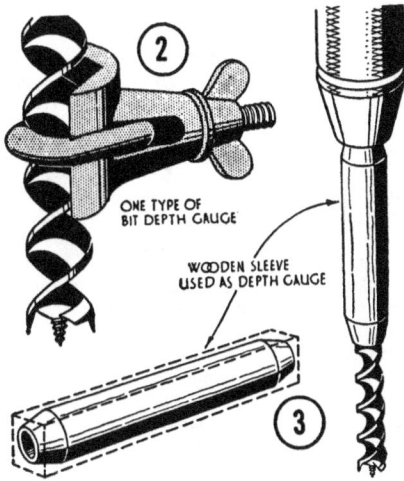

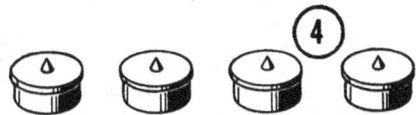

type of which is in Figure 1. This comes with a set of interchangeable guides or bushings for different sizes of auger bits. Although ⅜" dowels are the ones most commonly used, the jig is equally adaptable for boring holes as small as 3/16" and as large as ¾".

Lines are squared across the work at the locations of the dowel holes. If both joining parts are marked in one operation, the lines are certain to coincide. The jig is now clamped on one piece with its index mark exactly on one of the lines previously drawn. The required guide or bushing is inserted in its holder, which is a V-block that slides back and forth. This is next adjusted so that the hole will be centered or at any desired distance from the edges. The guide is then fastened with a thumb screw.

When the hole is bored, the guide not only directs the bit unfailingly to the right starting point, but keeps it perfectly vertical. The jig is then unclamped and moved to the next line for boring another hole. No further adjustment is needed.

When all the dowel holes have been bored in one piece, the operation is repeated on the other. The only necessary precaution is to mark the face of each piece distinctly and take care to keep the unmarked side toward you at all times so that the clamping screw of the jig always bears against the non-face side of the work. Then it doesn't matter particularly if the guide is centered on the edge or not, because all the holes will be precisely the same distance from the face anyway.

ble, especially as the exact spacing or position of the dowels usually does not matter a great deal.

One way is to use a set of what are called "dowel centers," which are illustrated in Fig. 4. These are obtainable in various sizes at small cost from craftwork supply houses and the larger hardware stores. The procedure is to bore the dowel holes into one piece, spacing them by eye. The bit preferably should have some sort of depth gauge and, of course, the holes should be bored straight. While the latter also can be done by eye and by sighting with a try square from time to time, a foolproof method will be described a little later.

Into the bored holes are inserted dowel centers of the correct size. The two parts which are to be joined are now placed in the proper position for assembly and pressed hard together. The sharp points of the dowel centers will mark the second piece so that it can be bored to match the first.

If dowel centers cannot readily be obtained, the same result can be obtained by driving small brads part way into one piece where the dowel holes are to be

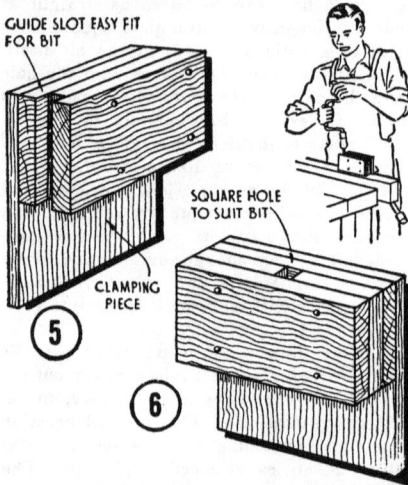

bored. The brads are cut off with cutting pliers so that only about ⅛" projects. The other piece is then placed in its correct relationship, and pressed hard so that the brads will mark the dowel-hole centers in it. The brads are pulled out and the boring is done in both parts as before.

In some cases even this trouble may be avoided. If one part to be joined can be held level in the vise, it is sufficient to lay ordinary household pins on the edge with their heads marking the points where the dowels are to be used. The second board is then carefully lowered on the first without disturbing the pins and pressed hard. The heads of the pins will mark the dowel centers in both edges simultaneously. This requires more manual dexterity than using brads, but is somewhat quicker.

Other methods of accomplishing the same result include cardboard or metal templates or wooden jigs. These are useful if many similar parts have to be doweled, but sufficient has been said to show that locating the holes should be no great problem.

To return to the question of boring the holes straight: A guide can be made in a few minutes by nailing together four scrap pieces of thin wood or plywood as shown in Fig. 5. This is placed on the board to be bored at the desired point and both are clamped together in the vise as indicated. In making cupboard doors and the like, old-time carpenters would sometimes use a waste end of one of the grooved stiles in exactly the same way. The open groove or slot makes a perfectly good guide if care is taken in boring, but it is not much more trouble to construct a closed jig as shown in Fig. 6.

In much work, where only short dowels are required, guides may be dispensed with because even the beginner can bore shallow holes sufficiently straight for this purpose. When used mainly as an aid in assembling a project, the dowels can be quite short. As a matter of fact, modern glues are so strong and withstand atmospheric changes so well that glued joints, if properly made, are stronger than the wood itself. Dowels and other fasteners are mere auxiliaries in well-glued work and therefore can be reduced to a minimum in both size and number.

Hints on Using Dowel Pins

WOODEN dowel pins should fit tightly in the holes bored for them—so tightly that they are difficult to insert unless the ends have been slightly pointed.

Many amateur craftsmen now buy dowels which are already cut to length, pointed at both ends and grooved. These are readily available, at least in the ⅜" size, from large craftwork dealers. However, plain dowel rods are still used by many woodworkers, and these craftsmen have to point the dowels themselves. The best way to do this is by hammering the end as shown in Fig. 1 to compress the wood. When the dowels are glued, the moisture from the glue causes the wood fibers to expand and the end of the dowel

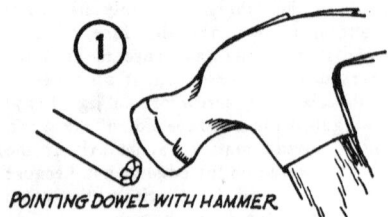

POINTING DOWEL WITH HAMMER.

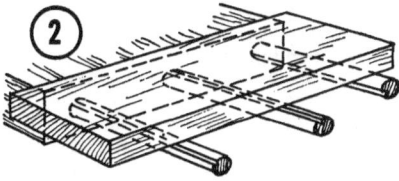

GAUGE FOR CUTTING OFF DOWELS

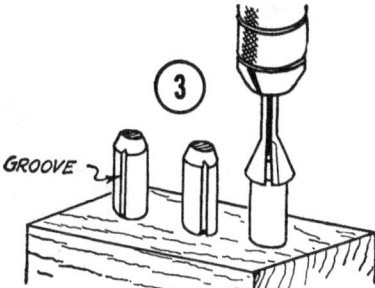

GROOVE

DOWEL SHARPENER

unsuitable. A tool especially made for this purpose is known as a dowel sharpener, Fig. 3, which is used in a bit brace. If not available, a coarse file may be used.

A well-fitting wooden dowel, if not grooved, will act like a piston in a cylinder and exert so much pressure when driven that it may cause the wood to split. To avoid this danger, some commercial dowel pins have spiral and lengthwise grooves, as shown in Fig. 4. Craft supply houses stock these in the $\frac{3}{8}$" size, $1\frac{1}{2}$" to 3" long.

When plain dowels are used, it is sufficient to provide a single lengthwise groove to allow the glue and air to escape (Fig. 3). To save the time required to cut such grooves, some woodworkers merely run a fine-set plane along each dowel stick before cutting it into short lengths. Taking a shaving off in this way leaves the dowel slightly flat and thus provides an escape

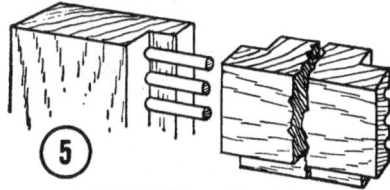

returns to its normal size. If, however, a dowel is pointed by removing some wood, the gluing area is reduced to a slight extent.

Dowels would be much more effective, in fact, if some convenient method could be devised to compress them uniformly all over. This is done commercially by a new process which squeezes square wooden rods under tremendous pressure to fit round dowel holes. The moisture in the glue expands the dowels, which grip the wood in the strongest and most durable type of doweled joint ever made.

When dowels of varied lengths are glued into holes, it is necessary to cut them off uniformly. A piece of wood, the width of which equals the desired projection of the dowels, may be used as in Fig. 2 to serve as a gauge. To point the ends of the dowels, the hammering method is, of course,

RABBETED JOINT WITH DOWELS GLUED IN STILE

passage for glue and air. However, as little wood as possible should be removed because the flat area reduces the effective gluing surface and, to that extent, weakens the joint, as can be seen in Fig. 4.

Another interesting and often debated question in regard to dowel joints is whether to insert and glue the dowels into the rails (cross members) first or into the stiles of a furniture frame, door or other part. They are usually placed in the rails first, but in the case of rabbeted joints such as the one shown in Fig. 5, some craftsmen believe the parts will draw up better when clamped if the dowels are first placed in the stiles. The dowel holes for a joint of this particular type are bored before the rabbeting is done.

SPIRAL DOWEL PIN

DOWEL FLATTENED TO ALLOW GLUE AND AIR TO ESCAPE

IF TOO WIDE, FLAT REDUCES STRENGTH OF JOINT

GROOVED AND FLATTENED DOWELS

Pinning Joints with Dowels

DOWELS can sometimes be used at an angle to reinforce joints in either old or new work. Suppose, for example, that several large frames have to me made for bulletin boards or other purposes and that it is desirable to use mitered joints for a

Through Dowels
(To be cut off flush later)

Temporary
Nail

Glued
Miter
Joint

①

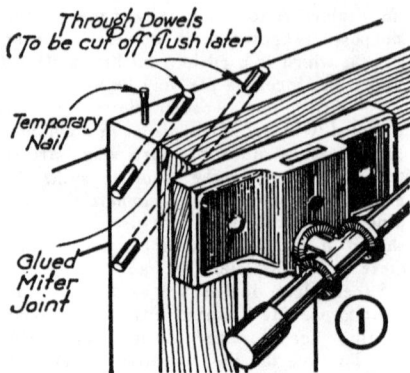

neat, workmanlike appearance. The pieces can be mitered and glued in the usual way and held temporarily either with small finishing nails or clamps. If nails are used, be sure to keep them well to one side or out of the way of the dowel holes, which now have to be bored as indicated in Fig. 1. They go through the corner and across the joint at right angles.

For average work, ⅜″ dowels are suitable, but larger or smaller dowels may be used according to the thickness of the stock being joined. The ¼″ size is best for ½″ to ⅜″ work; and the ½″ diameter is recommended for rails ranging from 1⅛″ to 1⅜″. After the glue has set, the projecting ends of the dowels are cut off flush.

With modifications, the same method may be used to make small paneled doors. As shown in Fig. 2, the stiles and rails are grooved in the usual way for the panel. To fit the grooves in the stiles, short tenons are cut on the ends of the rails. The doors are then assembled with glue and held with clamps. Slanting holes are next bored into the top and bottom edges so that dowels may be inserted as in Fig. 2. Note that in this case the holes are not continued

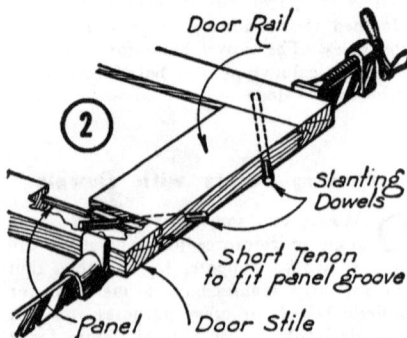

Door Rail

②

Slanting
Dowels

Short Tenon
to fit panel groove

Panel   Door Stile

through the front and back edges of the door, where they might prove unsightly.

The slanting dowels hold surprisingly well—so well, in fact, that the clamps may be removed at once and used for other work, if necessary. It is desirable, of course, to use as heavy dowels as the thickness of the rails and stiles will permit.

New Dowels Expand When Glued

ONE of the most remarkable modern developments in woodworking joints—the expanding dowel—is just becoming available to amateur craftsmen. Few professional woodworkers and hardly any amateurs have used these new dowels as yet. They look somewhat like ordinary spiral-grooved dowel pins and come in a variety of diameters and in lengths from 1″ up, but the grooves or serrations are much finer and run lengthwise. Both ends are pointed.

The secret of the dowels lies in the way they are manufactured—a patented method. The dowel stock used is 1/16″ larger than the size hole the dowels are to fit; that is, ⅜″ expanding dowels are made from 7/16″ dowel stock. However, no wood is removed. The dowels are serrated and the ends pointed by compression. They therefore enter the holes readily, allow any excess glue to escape along the serrations, but then expand because of the moisture in the glue.

The holding power of the new dowels is claimed to be 100 percent greater than ordinary dowels. No amount of dry weather and heat will cause the dowels to become loose. If insufficient glue is applied, it makes little difference, since there is no danger of what is called a "starved" joint. Furthermore, the dowels slip readily into the holes so that there is hardly any likelihood that they will split the wood, which may happen when ordinary dowels, which must fit tightly, are forced into place.

Since the dowels are easier to use, if anything, than ordinary ones, no special precautions are needed. However, the choice of glue is very important. Many tests, according to the manufacturers, indicate that best results are obtained by using liquid hide glue.

Wooden Dowel Gauge Fits Over Joint Then It Locates Hole and Guides Bit

THE USE of this gauge in locating dowel holes which are to be bored by hand will save gauging the distance from the face of the stock and will automatically insure accuracy in boring matching holes in both members of the joint. The gauge will also act as a guide in boring each hole perpendicular.

The gauge consists of five pieces of wood; a core piece is fitted with two guide strips on each side. The core has a vertical hole for the bit and a horizontal hole for expelling shavings. The gauge illustrated is made to fit $\frac{3}{4}''$ stock. Other sizes, also, can be made.

The gauge is made by boring hole (C) of desired size—the hole should match the size of bit to be used—through

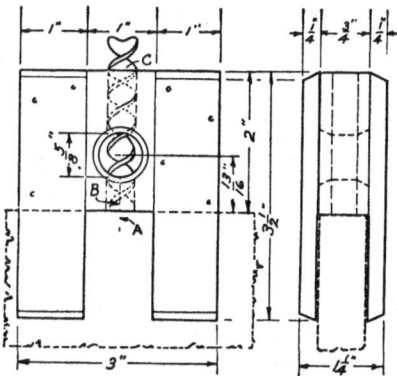

the $\frac{3}{4}''$x2''x3'' block. This may be done by hand, although a drill press is more accurate. In boring the dowel hole the shavings will escape through the $\frac{5}{8}$ double countersunk hole. Four pieces $\frac{1}{4}''$x1''x3$\frac{1}{2}''$ are glued and bradded in place to straddle the joint member. The mark (A) is made on each board to indicate the location of each dowel. The gauge is moved along the board until the center mark (B) of the gauge coincides with mark (A) on the board. The bit dropped through hole (C) will be correctly centered.

Steel Dowels for Small Work

IN MAKING small projects where the wood is thin, nails can sometimes be used to advantage instead of wooden dowels. The head ends are cut from the nails and the blunt ends are then driven into small lead holes drilled into one of the members to be joined, as in Fig. 1. Glue is applied and the other member is pressed into place and clamped tight. If the sharp projecting ends of the nails will not penetrate the wood by pressure alone, holes can

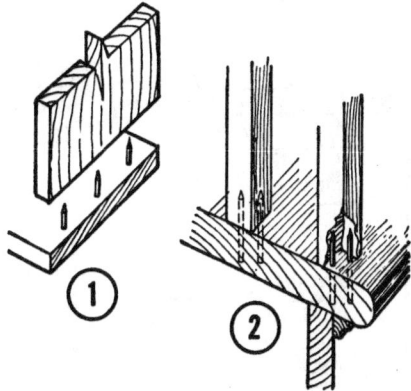

be drilled where the points of the nails have left their marks.

This method is occasionally used even for larger work, as when fastening stair-rail balusters to stair treads in rush work where there is no time to make better joints. The nails are set, points up, into holes drilled in the treads; then the balusters, if of soft wood such as white pine, are forced into place as indicated in Fig. 2. If the wood is harder, holes are drilled, just as for wooden dowels.

Laying Out Mortises and Tenons

THE REAL secret of constructing a piece of furniture that will stay together may be found in the joints that are used to assemble the various members. One of the most commonly used joints on tables and chairs is the mortise and tenon. These joints must be laid out properly and cut accurately if they are to live up to their reputation for strength, rigidity and long service. Even

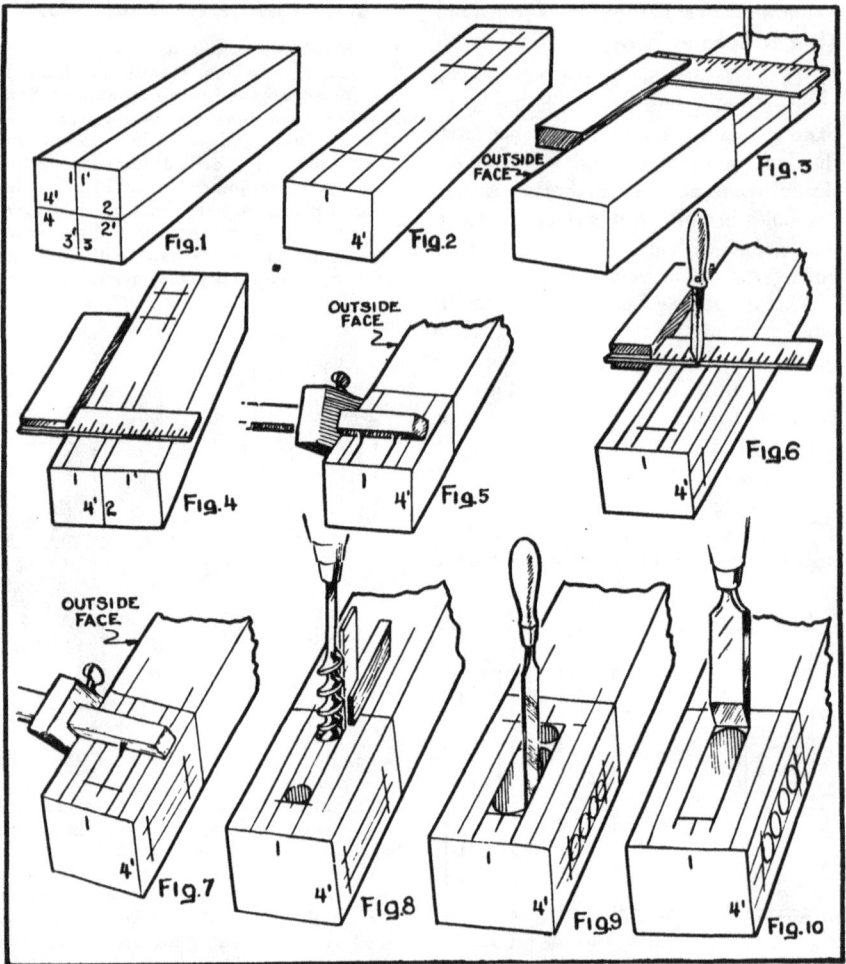

Fig.1 | Fig.2 | Fig.3 | Fig.4 | Fig.5 | Fig.6 | Fig.7 | Fig.8 | Fig.9 | Fig.10

more important than precision line cutting of the joint is the exactness of location and size of the layout and the identical transfer of the layout from one member to another.

The first step in laying out a mortise is to establish its position on the stock. Fig. 1 shows four pieces of stock which may be chair or table legs. The relative position of each leg is established by placing all four of them together and marking the adjacent sides as shown with 1—1', 2—2' and so on. It is on these marked sides that the mortise is to be located. Fig. 2 shows the establishing of the rails and stretchers on one face of the leg. The location of these members should be obtained from a working drawing. It is within these layouts that the mortise must be located. Sometimes a drawing shows the exact size of the mortise, but if these dimensions are lacking, the mortise should be laid out within the limits of the stretchers and rails so as to allow for a shoulder on each side of the tenon.

Fig. 3 shows how the limits of the stretchers and rails are carried over to the adjacent side by means of a try-square, always with the handle on the outside face. Fig. 4 shows how the limits of the stretchers and rails are carried over from one piece to another. This is a better method than trying to repeat the dimension with a rule. In Fig. 5 a mortise gauge is used to scribe the parallel lines which are the limits of the mortise. A knife is used, as in Fig. 6, to scribe the lines establishing the length of the mortise. With a marking gauge, a center line is drawn through the mortise as in Fig. 7.

An auger bit of the size equivalent to the width of the mortise is used to remove as much wood as possible. This is shown in Fig. 8. Figures 9 and 10 show how the chisel is used to remove waste wood and cut the mortise square.

MORTISE-AND-TENON PROPORTIONS

THE mortise-and-tenon joint is often used in fine cabinetwork. Unless the craftsman is following definite plans, he is often at a loss to know the correct proportions for such a joint. The following table should be referred to for the desirable measurements of the mortise and the tenon.

A	B	C
Thickness of Stock to be Mortised	Maximum Width of Mortise	Desirable Length of Tenon
1/2"	1/4"	5/8"
5/8"	5/16"	3/4"
3/4"	3/8"	1"
7/8"	3/8"	1"
1"	1/2"	1 1/4"
1 1/4"	1/2"	1 1/2"
1 1/2"	5/8"	1 3/4"
1 3/4"	3/4"	2"
2"	7/8"	2 1/2"

For any given thickness of stock such as is listed in column A, the width of the mortise should not exceed the dimension given in column B.

As a general rule, the mortise of a mortise-and-tenon joint is cut in the larger member. For best results

from the standpoint of obtaining a tight fit of the joint, the tenon should have shoulders on all four sides if practical; therefore, the thickness of the member on which the tenon is to be cut has a limiting factor on the width of the mortise as given in column B.

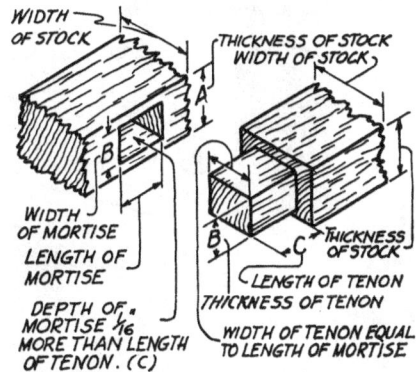

WIDTH OF STOCK
THICKNESS OF STOCK
WIDTH OF STOCK
WIDTH OF MORTISE
LENGTH OF MORTISE
DEPTH OF MORTISE 1/16 MORE THAN LENGTH OF TENON. (C)
LENGTH OF TENON
THICKNESS OF TENON
WIDTH OF TENON EQUAL TO LENGTH OF MORTISE

The length of the tenon as listed in column C and shown in the sketch is the most desirable one, but it is sometimes limited by the width of the stock in which the mortise has been cut. If the width of the stock is too small to cut the mortise to a depth that will take the tenon length listed in column C, then a stub or shortened tenon will have to be made. The length of the mortise is limited by the width of the tenon. The tenon width should allow for shoulders on each side. Single mortises of great lengths should be avoided.

The proper way to cut a mortise-and-tenon joint is to cut the mortise first, then make the tenon to fit the mortise. Any trimming that is done to fit the two parts together should be done on the cheeks of the tenon rather than on the sides of the mortise.

Haunched Joints in Furniture

MANY amateur cabinetmakers have at least a vague notion as to what a so-called "haunched" mortise-and-tenon joint is, but do not understand its purposes and therefore never bother to use it.

The haunched joint, which is shown in several forms, is designed to resist any tendency of one member to twist in relation to the other. If a tenon is made as wide as the rail, apron, stile or other member in which it is cut, it will keep the piece from twisting, but the trouble

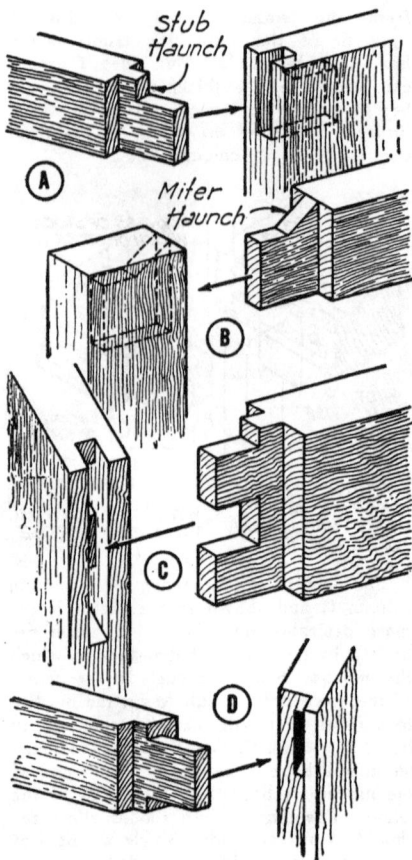

Stub Haunch

A

Miter Haunch

B

C

D

and-tenon; that is, with a long and short shoulder for rabbeted frame members, as in Fig D, or "barefaced" where there is a shoulder on only one side of the tenon of good furniture.

Trick Joint Is Very Strong

IN BUILDING furniture with mortise-and-tenon joints, it frequently happens that the mortises in two adjacent sides of a post run into each other at the center of the post, as shown in Fig. 1. In this case the ends of the tenons are cut on a 45° angle, otherwise one tenon would have to be cut shorter than the other to prevent the ends from interfering.

Amateur cabinetmakers who enjoy unusual and tricky joints can solve this problem in another and better way—one that

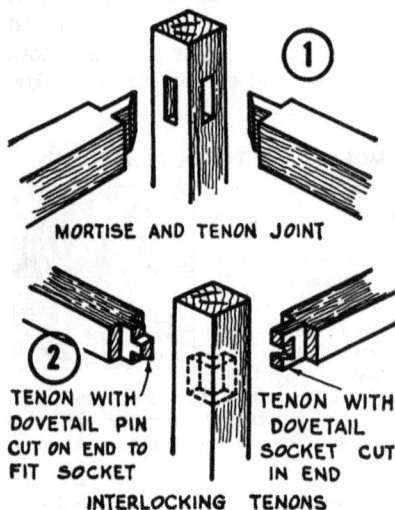

1

MORTISE AND TENON JOINT

2

TENON WITH DOVETAIL PIN CUT ON END TO FIT SOCKET

TENON WITH DOVETAIL SOCKET CUT IN END

INTERLOCKING TENONS

very few woodworkers have ever encountered. It is a method of making a concealed dovetail on the end of the tenons in such a way that one rail locks the other.

The tenons are made in the usual way to fill the mortises completely. Then, instead of mitering the ends, a dovetail pin is cut on one tenon and a dovetail socket in the other as shown in Fig. 2. If the fitting is carefully done, the tenons will mesh when in place and, if properly glued, will provide a very strong and durable joint. It is particularly good for frameworks which are left open and unbraced, as a serving table on wheels, a portable bar or any piece of furniture which is moved around and subjected to considerable strain.

is that the corresponding mortise may weaken the adjoining piece too much. Therefore a compromise is made, and part of the tenon is greatly reduced in length so that it becomes merely a stub as shown at A.

If used in a conspicuous location where the stub would show in the other piece, the joint is modified by cutting a miter as shown at B. In each case, of course, the mortise is cut to match.

Where the rail or other tenoned member is very wide, the arrangement shown at C may be followed. This is one type of double mortise-and-tenon joint, and it is also haunched for the reason mentioned. From the construction standpoint, it can be regarded as a single full-width tenon which has been cut away to form two tenons and two haunches.

These joints can, of course, be varied in as many ways as an ordinary mortise-

Simplified Way to Cut Box Corners

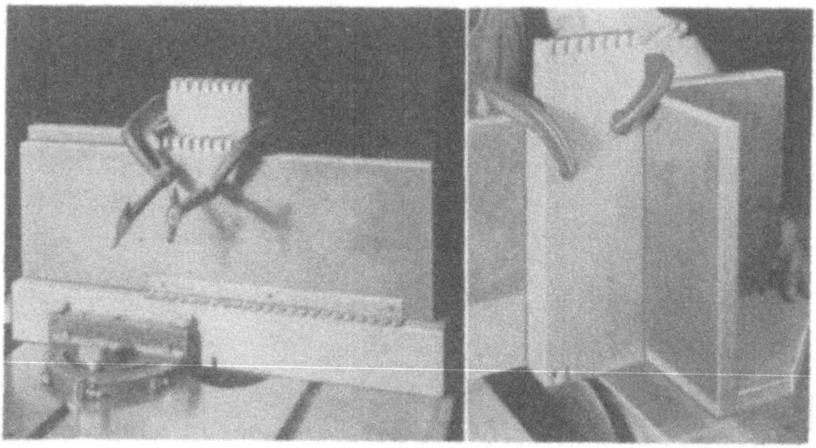

DRAWER construction usually involves either a dovetail or a box-corner joint. Of the two joints, the box-corner, sometimes known as the finger-lap joint, is much the simpler and quicker to make when a bench saw jig as shown here is made up first.

The first requisite is an absolutely straight facing piece (A) to be fastened to the miter gauge. It should preferably be laminated and thoroughly coated with linseed oil to prevent warpage. The fixture or jig itself consists of a bracket assembly of ¾" plywood pieces, squared and securely glued and screwed together. The spacing comb is a piece of brass or iron angle with ¼" cuts. The same comb can be used to make ½" dovetails by using a ½" dado head and using every other notch in the comb. Extreme care must be used in laying out and cutting the slots in the comb. When making the saw cuts for the slots, saw away from the line and rely on filing and fitting to get a close fit on a No. 12 wood screw, used as a guide pin.

The No. 12 wood screw is driven into the top of the miter gauge facing piece (A) as indicated, which is in line with the left-hand side of the dado saw blade. Now place the fixture on the saw table, against (A)

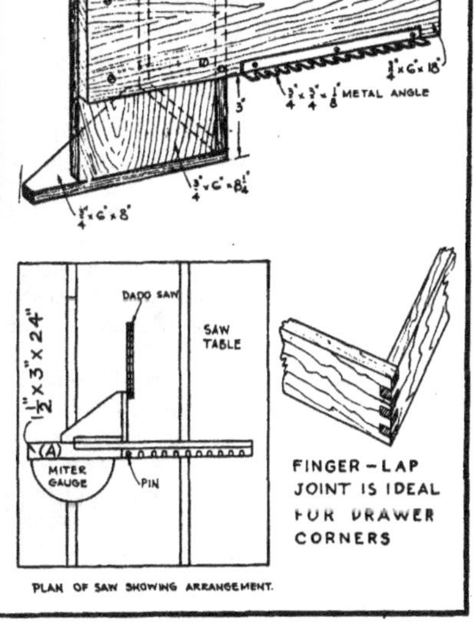

Center to center spacing on comb must be exactly twice the thickness of the dado saws
METAL ANGLE
DADO SAW
SAW TABLE
(A)
MITER GAUGE
PIN
PLAN OF SAW SHOWING ARRANGEMENT.

FINGER–LAP JOINT IS IDEAL FOR DRAWER CORNERS

and move it to the right until it rests against the side of the dado saw blade. Now place the comb on (A) with the slot on the extreme left of the comb engaging the screw. Then screw it fast to the crosspiece.

Since our spacing of the tenons of the joint are dependent on the thickness of the dado saws (which are usually ⅛″) then the width of our box sides should be a multiple of ⅛″ or ¼″, whichever we use. With the ¼″ comb, the drawer sides can be any ¼″ dimension such as 3¼″, 4½″, etc.

The four sides of a box may be cut together. The stock is placed in the fixture with the left-hand edges firmly against the fixture and the ends resting squarely on the saw table, in which position they are clamped.

Starting with the comb engaging the screw at such a point as to intercept the right-hand edge of the stock, run the stock over the saw blade. The height of the saw blade above the table should be equal to the thickness of one piece of stock. Now draw the fixture back, move it to the right one slot, run it over the saw and repeat until the last cut has been made. Release the clamps and turn the stock end for end, keeping the same edges to the left, and repeat the procedure.

You will find that by reversing two of the finished pieces edge for edge, they will match up.

Reinforcing Mitered Frames

THERE are many ways to reinforce the mitered joints of picture frames, tray frames and other frames without using nails or screws. Most of these, such as the ones shown in Fig. 1, are familiar to the amateur cabinetmaker.

Two especially good methods of strengthening a plain mitered joint after it has been made are shown in Fig. 2. After the frame has been glued together, saw slots may be cut as at A to receive pieces of thick veneer, which are glued in and trimmed off later. In the second method shown at B, a dovetail groove is cut across the back of each corner after the glue has set, and

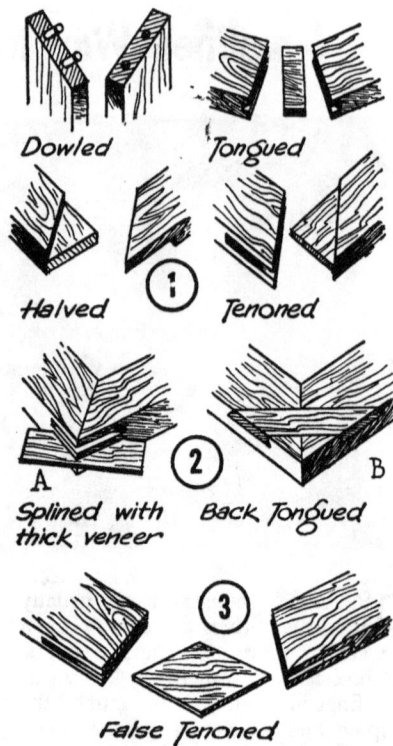

Dowled Tongued

Halved ① Tenoned

A ② B

Splined with thick veneer Back Tongued

③

False Tenoned

a strip of hardwood is fitted in, glued and afterwards trimmed flush.

A little-known variation of the mortise-and-tenon miter is shown in Fig. 3. In this case all the frame pieces have similar open mortises cut in them, which is quicker than cutting mortises in two frame members and tenons on the other two. Separate false tenons are then glued in. The grain of the false tenons should, of course, run across the mitered joints.

Hints on Making Miter Joints

WHEN it is necessary to join two pieces of different widths or thicknesses with a mitered joint, the simplest type to use is the so-called "stopped miter." The narrower or thinner piece is mitered in the usual way as shown at A, Fig. 1, and the wider or thicker piece is mitered to match, at B. The joint may be assembled with glue alone or reinforced with nails or screws, as required.

Since long mitered joints require very accurate machining to fit perfectly, it is easier in some instances to use the more

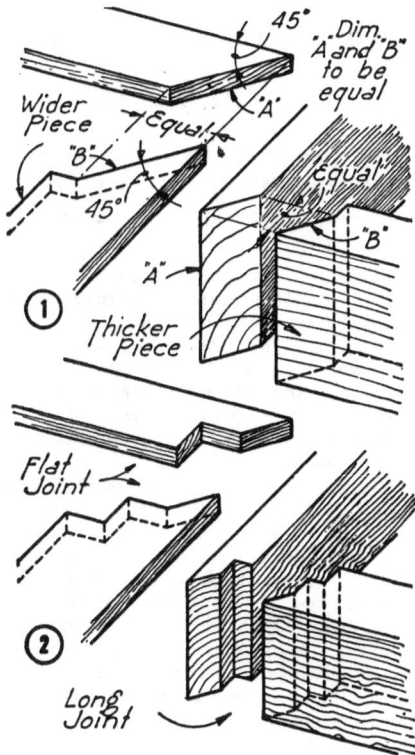

cut diagonally across the corner as in Fig. 2. A strip long enough to make all the required keys is then planed to fit the slots tightly. Pieces are cut off and glued into each slot and later trimmed flush.

The second method requires saw kerfs to be made as in Fig. 3. Pieces of veneer of a thickness to fit the kerfs are then glued

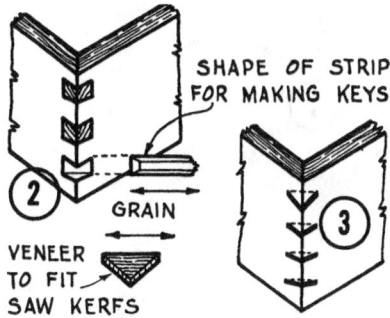

into them. Note that the upper and lower saw kerfs are slanted upward and downward respectively for additional strength.

From the standpoint of appearance, the joint shown in Fig. 2, if neatly made, is rather decorative as it resembles to some extent a handmade dovetail. The reinforcement shown in Fig. 3, although inconspicuous, is usually employed only when a face veneer is to be applied over the work, or the corners are to be trimmed with molding or overlays.

complicated dado-and-miter joint shown in Fig. 2. This is sometimes referred to as a "ledge-and-miter joint." It makes an excellent joint for boxes and chests.

Reinforcing Mitered Joints

WHEN mitered joints are used in constructing a box, chest or other projects, it is common practice to reinforce them with splines which have the grain running crosswise, as shown in Figure 1. This method, however, is not always the most convenient to use and sometimes it is out of the question, as, for example, in repair work where mitered joints require to be strengthened without taking them apart.

Two ways to reinforce mitered joints from the outside are illustrated in Figs. 2 and 3.

The first calls for dovetail slots to be

Corner Joints for Plywood

WHEN joining ¾" or other fairly thick plywood to form a modern cabinet, chest, box or other project, many woodworkers are content to use the common rabbeted joint shown in Fig. 1 on the following page. This forms a strong corner joint, but it involves difficulty in the finishing process, especially if a stained or natural finish, rather than a painted finish, is to be used. The comparatively wide end strip marked A consists partly of the core or interior layers of the plywood and takes the finish differently from the base of the veneer so that an ugly line is always visible. This is true whether the plywood has a lumber core a plywood core.

If the craftsman has a modern bench saw in good working condition and if the plywood panels are not too large to handle conveniently on the machine, it requires only a moderate amount of extra work to make the much superior joints shown in Figs. 2 and 3.

In Fig. 2, the exposed end of the plywood is much thinner and is also slightly rounded, which gives a far better finished

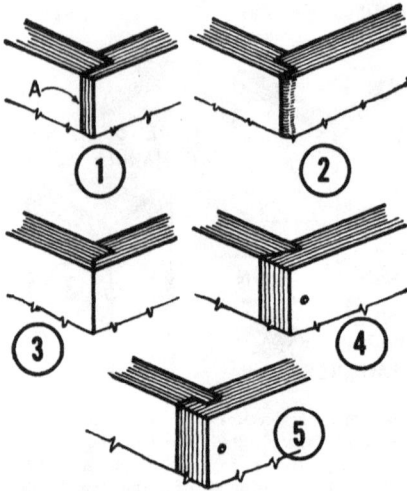

effect. At the same time, the gluing surfaces are adequate and designed to provide a strong, easily assembled joint. In Fig. 3, no end grain wood is visible, which makes the joint ideal from the finishing standpoint, although it is somewhat more difficult to machine and fit accurately.

In the construction of plywood projects where appearance is of less importance, but glued and nailed or screwed joints of the utmost strength are required, the joint shown in Fig. 4 is worthy of consideration. The nails or screws draw it tightly together and it then holds with a sort of dovetail effect. It is much better, for example, than the joint shown in Fig. 5.

Reinforced Plywood Joint

A N INCONSPIC-UOUS reinforced corner joint for use in plywood construction is shown in the accompanying sketch. The strengthening insert is made of hardwood and its principal purpose is to give a secure anchorage for the nails or screws which are used in assembling the project.

The Secret of Making Dovetails Quickly

You can easily win a reputation for craftsmanship—and have fun, too—by mastering this fine joint

DO HOME craftsmen use dovetail joints to any large extent? Perhaps your offhand answer would be "no." The dovetail joint is highly esteemed as the king of woodworking joints, but the general opinion is that it is difficult to make—and assuredly most woodworking textbooks and printed instructions on the joint make it appear so.

But why avoid the dovetail joint? If you have looked at much antique furniture, whether made by expert cabinetmakers for the parlor or built by the village carpenter for the kitchen, you must have noticed that dovetail joints were used extensively. Perhaps you have said to yourself, "What patience and skill these old woodworkers must have had!"

Nothing could be truer if those old-time workmen went about making dovetails in the way the average amateur does, but they didn't. They knew all sorts of tricks and short cuts to make the work easy. It was a practical, convenient everyday joint in their estimation.

Actually, the multiple hand dovetail is one of the finest and most beautiful woodworking joints ever devised. There is no quicker or easier way for an amateur to make a reputation for himself as an expert craftsman than by spending the time necessary to master the hand dovetail. It is well recognized as representing hand craftsmanship at its best.

There are several ways to make multiple dovetails. One is by using a special attachment on the drill press. Another is to use a dovetail attachment with an electric router.

The machine dovetail is a strong, efficient joint, but because of its even spacing and heavy appearance, it does not have the decorative quality of the handmade dovetail, as can be seen in Fig. 1. It is purely a utility joint and should be used more extensively by those home craftsmen who are fortunate enough to have the necessary equipment.

The hand dovetail, on the other hand,

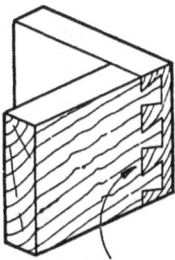

Machine-Type Multiple Lapped or Half-Blind Dovetail

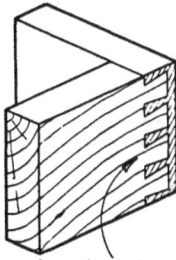

①

Hand-Made Multiple Through Dovetail

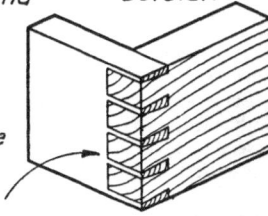

Handmade Multiple Lapped Dovetail

of making lapped dovetail joints between the two sides and the front of a drawer:

First, square the stock accurately to dimension and mark the working face and working edge of each. If the pieces are properly squared to begin with, you can mark the limits of the joint with the gauge instead of the try-square, which is faster.

Gauge lines very lightly across the ends of the front member to represent the amount the side members are to be lapped

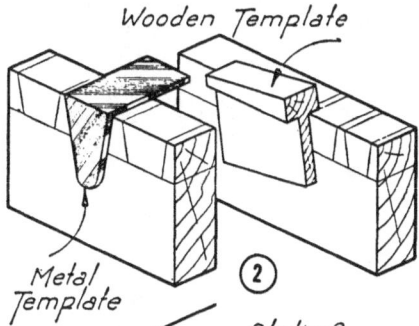

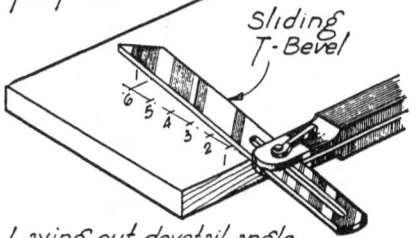

Wooden Template

Metal Template

②

Sliding T-Bevel

Laying out dovetail angle for making template. For ordinary dovetails use 1:6 angle for fine exposed joints use 1:8 angle

is such a decorative joint that it is frequently exposed to view. As it cannot be duplicated by machine, it always gives a piece of handmade quality which enhances its value.

To make hand dovetails with the speed and ease of old-time cabinetmakers, you will have to depend largely on your eye. After all, the joint is supposed to look as if it were made by hand and slight irregularities in the spacing and proportions add rather than detract from its decorative appearance. Also, you may as well ignore the technical terminology of dovetail joints. It is easier to think of a multiple dovetail joint as one in which the projecting parts of one member slip into sockets in the other member, or call one part the tenon piece and the other the mortise piece.

You can, if you wish, make a sheet metal or wooden template as shown in Fig. 2. The correct angle for ordinary dovetails is 1 to 6 as shown in Fig. .2, but for the best appearance in exposed work, the proportion of 1 to 8 is preferred.

The trick in making multiple dovetail joints quickly, however, is to spend as little time as possible in laying out the joints and learning to do the work mainly by eye. With practice you can soon get to make dovetail joints so expertly that you will wonder why you ever thought they were particularly difficult.

Here, for example, is one speedy method

into the front. If the front is ¾" thick, the gauge could be set for ½" or a little more. With the same setting, gauge lines lightly on the faces and edges of the side members at each end. Also, gauge 'the thickness of the side pieces across the inner face of the front piece at each end.

Now place all three pieces in the vise in the position shown in Fig. 3. Working by eye, divide the extending ends of the side pieces into the desired number of dovetails. Make the end division, as indicated in Fig. 3, somewhat wider than the other divisions. To be exact, you will probably want to square these lines across, and it is good practice to do so, but speed comes from working by eye without this aid. It is not difficult to keep the dovetail saw approximately square with the work.

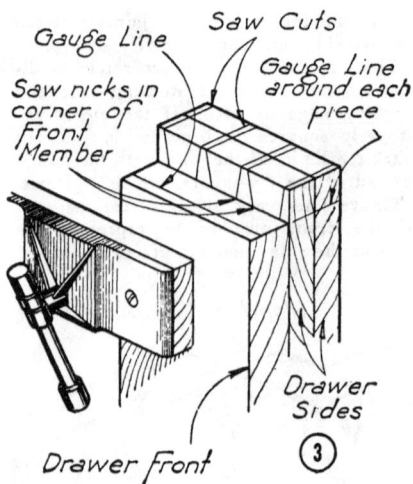

Saw Cuts

Gauge Line

Gauge Line around each piece

Saw nicks in corner of Front Member

Drawer Sides

Drawer Front

③

After chiseling Waste Wood

④

Drawer side in position for marking sockets on end of front member

⑤

Drawer Front (in vise)

remainder from the other side. The small waste pieces at each end of the joint can be removed with the dovetail saw. This stage of the work is shown in Fig. 4.

Replace the front member in the vise as shown in Fig. 5 and lay one of the finished sides on it in the correct position. Now mark the sockets by using a scribing awl, the small blade of your pocketknife, or a very hard, sharp pencil. As you gain experience, you may be able to omit this operation, because the corner of the drawer front has already been nicked with the saw sufficiently to indicate where to start cutting, and you can learn to judge the correct angle closely enough for all practical purposes. However, it takes a little time to do the marking.

Place an identifying mark or number on both pieces so that you will be able to assemble them in the same position without hesitation later on. Now make the saw cuts for the sockets as shown in Fig. 6, continuing them down to the lines previously gauged. Do the cutting on the side of the line which will be in the waste wood so as to insure a good fit.

Turn the stock end for end in the vise and mark the opposite end in exactly the same way, using the other finished side piece for this purpose. Again mark each piece so that the joints will be assembled as laid out. Make the last series of saw cuts in the same way. The sockets can then be chiseled to the correct depths, giving the results shown in Fig. 7.

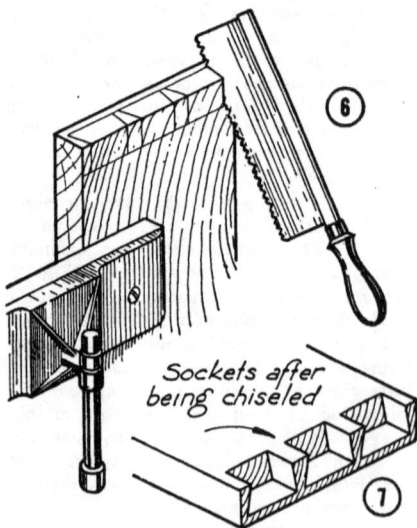

⑥

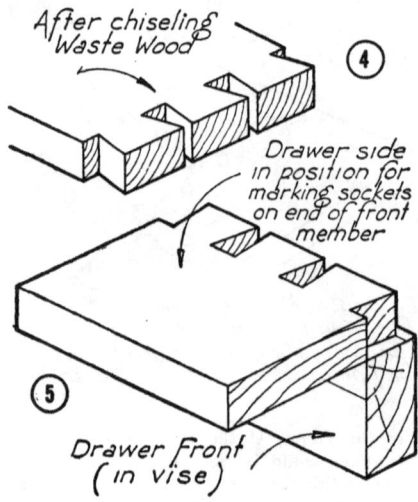

Sockets after being chiseled

⑦

On your first attempts, too, you can indicate the angles in pencil, but the idea is to learn to cut freehand. The exact angles are not particularly important.

With a dovetail saw or a small back saw, make the saw cuts as in Fig. 3. In finishing each, let the saw teeth score the corner of the front piece very slightly as shown.

Now you can remove the pieces and chisel the waste wood between the saw cuts already made in the side members. Use a small, very sharp bevel-edge chisel. Cut half the waste wood away from one side, then turn the board over and cut the

Make a trial assembly. Some additional fitting may be required, but with practice you will be surprised how well and quickly dovetail joints made in this way will go together.

When making an open or "through" multiple dovetail, the same general procedure may be followed. In making a box, for example, both ends of two of the pieces can first be cut as shown in Fig. 8. Before doing any chiseling, mark the ends of the other two pieces with the saw as shown in Fig. 9. In each case, complete the saw cuts immediately before removing the stock from the vise, but be sure to do the actual sawing in what will be the waste wood.

Once you discover for yourself how this method speeds up the work, you will understand why old-time woodworkers did not look on dovetailing as much of a chore and. therefore, used this fine joint so frequently.

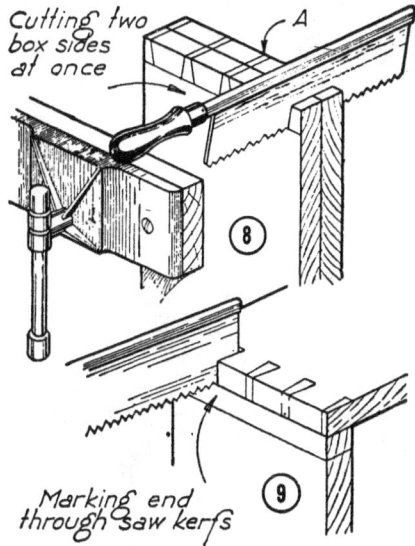

Cutting two box sides at once

Marking end through saw kerfs

Blind Dovetail and Miter Joint

OF ALL the various types of dovetail joints, the most difficult to lay out and cut is the blind dovetail and miter. This joint is used in the construction of chests or drawers on the better class of furniture because it produces a corner showing no end grain but having a great deal of strength. There is, in reality, nothing difficult in its construction, if the time is taken to work out the joint properly. It is a joint that is seldom found in commercial furniture and is therefore all the more a mark of distinction on a piece of home-made furniture. Requiring some skill and more diligence to execute, the craftsman who employs it will leave a fine testimonial of his work and extend the life of his project.

The number of fingers will vary with the width of the wood that the joint is to be cut in as well as the size of the fingers themselves. With this kept in mind, the construction of the joint may be broken down and analyzed as follows:

Sketch No. 1 shows the first lay-out and first cuts that are made at the ends of both pieces of stock. This consists of a miter cut across the upper and lower edges, ¼" deep. The shoulder is then cleaned with a sharp chisel. The second cut is made on the circular saw by setting the table at an angle of 45 degrees with the blade set for a depth of ¼". This will make the cut on the end at the proper angle. The shoulder, as shown in Fig. 1, is cut on the circular saw with the table at an angle of 90 degrees. The saw blade will have to be set so that it will just meet the miter cut. These cuts will form the wood into the shape shown in Fig. 2.

As was mentioned, the number of grooves and fingers will vary, but for the sake of illustration, the sketches shown have four and three, and three and four respectively. Sketch No. 3 shows the layout of the left and right pieces. It is advisable to complete the layout of the left side first, as shown, then carry over to the other piece the measurements as found on the first layout. A-1 should correspond with

23

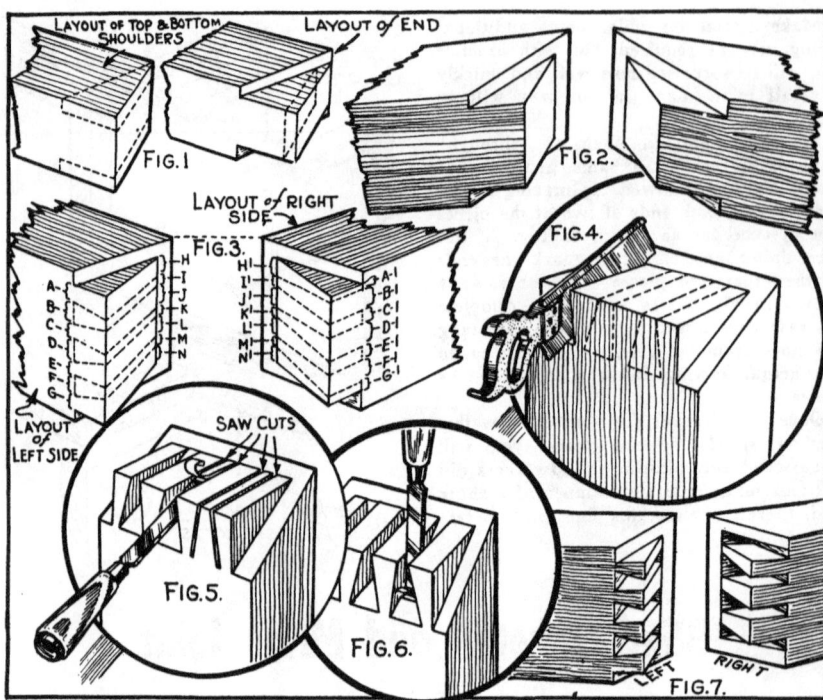

FIG. 1 — LAYOUT OF TOP & BOTTOM SHOULDERS

LAYOUT OF END

FIG. 2.

LAYOUT OF RIGHT SIDE

FIG. 3.

FIG. 4.

LAYOUT OF LEFT SIDE

SAW CUTS

FIG. 5.

FIG. 6.

LEFT   RIGHT

FIG. 7.

A, B-1 with B and so on down the line. H-1 at the other end of the block corresponds to H and so on.

Up to this point, a great deal of skill in handling tools is not required but that isn't the case when cutting out the joint itself. Here extreme care must be taken and without tools in the proper condition, a great deal of difficulty will be encountered. Fig. 4 shows the use of the back saw to make the first cut in forming the groove and finger. The one point to keep in mind when performing this operation is to saw on the side of the line where the stock is to be removed. If this is overlooked, the joint will be loose. The saw is not held square to the end of the stock, but must be slanted to conform with the lines of the joint. Fig. 5 shows the use of a chisel to clean out the grooves. This operation leaves the bottom of the groove at an angle of 45 degrees. Fig 6 is the last step in the construction of the joint. This consists of squaring up the inside corner with the chisel. The finished joint is shown in Fig. 7

Ways of Marking and Cutting Joints Accurately

GEOMETRY teaches that a line has neither width nor thickness. Perhaps so, but many craftsmen produce lines for joint layouts so wide that accurate joining is not possible. Glue is not a substitute for close fitting; a joint that rattles will not remain tight for long, while a well fitted one glued properly will stand for fifty to one hundred years.

There is one right way to cut to a line for joint work. Use a light pencil for the general squaring, especially around a table leg, to avoid sanding out lines later, but for the lines which are to be cut, go over with a sharp knife, scoring by repeated use of knife to a depth of at least $\frac{1}{16}''$. Use a square in this work.

At a distance of about $\frac{1}{8}''$ to $\frac{1}{4}''$ from the scored line, on that part of wood to be removed, cut into the scored line with the knife to produce a groove with one edge vertical. This vertical edge is the line of saw cut; place the saw tightly against the vertical edge and cut.

For fine work with chisel, lay out the cut in the same manner, sinking the knife point in the corners and cutting from the corners outward. This method will prevent the chisel from backing into the wood beyond the line, especially in soft wood. Mortise and tenon cuts made this way will be perfect without trimming. One cause of poor tenon cutting is the use of the common back saw for cutting with the grain. The fine teeth cut and filed for cross cutting make too wide

a kerf. Every artisan should own a 14- to 18-inch back saw with teeth cut and filed for ripping, with 12 to 16 teeth per inch.

Instead of using a knife when marking for a cut with the grain where a square edge is available for guiding the gauge, use the marking gauge with pins filed for cutting. Marking gauges as they come from the manufacturer have rounded pins, unsuitable for accurate marking. Remove the pin and file to a taper about $\frac{1}{2}''$ from the end and thin enough so that pin is not over $\frac{1}{16}''$ thick at a distance of $\frac{3}{16}''$ from the end. Finish similar to a knife point. File so that the leading edge, when pushing the gauge from you is sharp for a distance of $\frac{3}{16}''$ from the end and the back edge is as thin as possible without danger of bending. Finish on a stone to a keen edge.

Ways to Tighten Loose Joints on Used Furniture

WHEN a chair or table develops loose joints it is not sufficient to pour a large quantity of glue in the space between the members and expect a tight joint. The theory of gluing is that the glue should enter the pores of the wood with the result that thousands of fine threads of glue form a cross binding as shown in the first sketch. This can be accomplished only with a joint that is tight to begin with and one that is free from dust and dirt. For this reason, a joint which is going to be glued together must never be sandpapered, stained, painted or oiled.

Joining surfaces should be cleaned thoroughly to remove all traces of glue. This must be done with a knife, scraper, chisel or wire brush, but under no circumstances should sandpaper be used as the dust and grit will be forced into the pores of the wood. If after the cleaning of joining members it is found that the joint is still fitting together snugly glue

GLUE THREADS

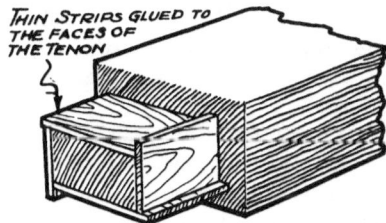

THIN STRIPS GLUED TO THE FACES OF THE TENON

may be applied to the joint and the work assembled and clamped with reasonable assurance that a successful repair job will be the result.

If the joint is found to be loose, either before it is clean or after, there should be no attempt made to assemble the work until these joints are made tight. In general it will be found that chairs and tables are assembled with either of two joints. They are a mortise and tenon or a dowel joint. In cases where the rails or rungs of a chair are round, in all probability the ends of these rungs are cut down to form the dowel which fits into the leg. The method employed when tightening this joint is a little different from that used for the mortise and tenon or the dowel joint and will be discussed later.

In order to tighten a mortise and tenon joint the tenon will have to be built up by gluing thin strips of wood to each of the four sides as shown in the second sketch. After these strips have been glued in place and the glue has set, the tenon can be trimmed down to fit the mortise. If the tenon has been found to be badly worn it may be necessary to true the faces of it with a chisel before applying the thin strips.

A piece of furniture that has been put together with dowel joints may have the dowels fitting loosely in the joining member. These dowels should be discarded. New ones may be turned to the proper diameter on the lathe to fit the holes in both members after they have been drilled out to same size.

In case of the round rail or rung there is no satisfactory method of making the rung larger but it is possible to reduce the size of the hole in the leg into which the rung fits. A plug or dowel should be turned to such a diameter that will fit in the hole. The plug should be glued in the hole and after the glue has been given time to set, the projecting end of the plug is dressed down to the shape of the leg. In the center of this plug a hole is bored the same diameter as the dowel on the end of the rung. After this operation the rung of the chair is glued into place and clamped.

Spline Joint Salvages Leftover Pieces of Plywood

IF YOU have been working with veneered panels or plywood, you probably have some odd-size pieces lying around the shop. These pieces which are left over when large panels are cut should always be saved as it is a simple matter to join them together to make a sheet of useful size. This can easily be done with half-inch thickness or larger, and even with three-ply quarter-inch thickness.

The first thing to do is to match the various pieces together according to their grain so that there will not be too much of a break in the figure where two pieces meet. Edges to be joined should be planed to fit perfectly, and the pieces should be so that they can be identified when the time comes for assembly.

The plywood is joined by the groove and spline method which provides a

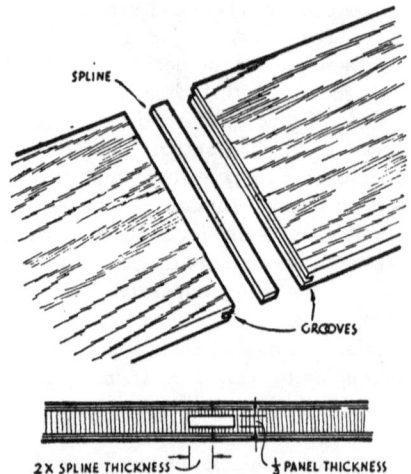

SPLINE

GROOVES

2X SPLINE THICKNESS   ½ PANEL THICKNESS

good tight joint. Using a circular saw, carefully cut a groove in the center of the edges to be joined. Hold the good face of every panel against the ripping fence and be sure the panel is always truly vertical to the plane of the saw table. Make the cut slowly and pres the panel at all times firmly against the fence. The best way to do this is to hold a straight board against the bottom edge of the panel as it is moved over the saw table. In this way you will be able to push the plywood over the blade with the right hand and at the same time hold it firmly against the fence by pressing the board against the panel with the other hand.

After the grooves have been made, a spline should be cut thick enough to fit tightly in the groove without springing it open. Since the spline supplies most of the strength in this joint, be sure it is cut from strong, clear material. It should be made just wide enough to fill the grooves when the pieces are assembled.

Apply either hot or cold glue to the spline and the grooves and assemble the pieces. Now draw the joints up tightly with clamps and remove all excess glue before it hardens on the surface. Protect the edges of the plywood from the clamps with strips of wood and keep the panels flat by clamping them to straight boards with hand screws. On thin panels it will sometimes be necessary to clamp flat pieces of wood above and below the joint to keep the surfaces from rising under the pressure. In this case cover the joint with paper so that the strips of wood will not be glued to the panels. Allow the glue to dry thoroughly and then even up the surface at the joint with a hand scraper and fine sandpaper held on a block. Do not do any more sanding than is absolutely necessary to even the joint, as it is very easy to cut through the surface veneer.

The joint will be hardly noticeable if the wood has been carefully matched and accurately fitted. It would seem that a panel joined in this way would be weaker at the seam, but this is not at all true. The panel will be strong enough to be used for any purpose where plywood is commonly employed.

Besides its use in saving waste material, this method is often very useful when matching and centering the figure on ready-made veneered panels. If the figure is not properly centered, a strip can very often be cut from one side and then joined to the other side. When ordering plywood or cutting the large size for use, remember that the small pieces can be joined. In this way it will often be possible to save considerable material which would otherwise be wasted.

When to Use Coped Joints

ALTHOUGH moldings are usually mitered at a right-angle corner where two pieces join, a miter joint is not always the best one for the purpose. If the corner is an interior one, a so-called "coped" joint is usually to be preferred.

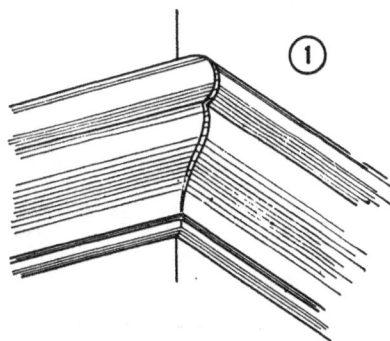

Mitered Picture Molding with ugly open joint

Common examples, which almost every amateur woodworker is likely to encounter at some time or the other, are where a new quarter-round base molding or base shoe has to be fitted around a room, or a picture molding has to be installed.

The reason an ordinary miter joint is undesirable in such work is because the shrinkage of the wood may cause the joint to open as shown in Fig. 1. A coped joint, where the end of one molding is cut

27

This molding cut square

This molding coped to fit against the other

②

Coped joint gives tighter appearance

Miter Cut

③

Coping line

Molding cut on miter to give coping line

Square-cut Quarter-round

Coped Quarter-round ④

Small, simple molding coped with knife

When to Use Bridle Joints

WOODWORKERS become so accustomed to using mortise-and-tenon joints that they are likely to overlook the special advantages of certain other types of joints. One of these is the so-called "bridle" joint—a sort of reversed mortise-and-tenon. Its function in furniture building and other cabinetmaking is to provide a joint between a vertical and a horizontal member when it is necessary, for the best appearance, to have the grain of the vertical part run uninterruptedly to the very end of the part.

One common example arises in constructing certain types of console tables with elliptical, semicircular or other odd-shaped tops. It may then be necessary to join a leg to a curved rail at some point other than the ends. If the table leg were fastened to the rail by means of a mortise-and-tenon joint, as shown in Fig. 1, the leg would appear to stop under the rail, and this would be particularly bad if the leg

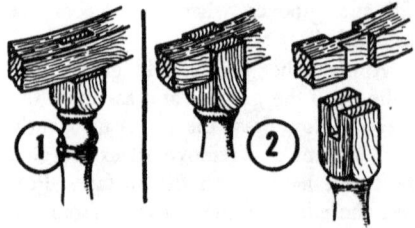

① ②

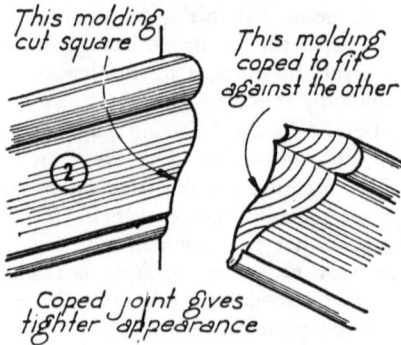

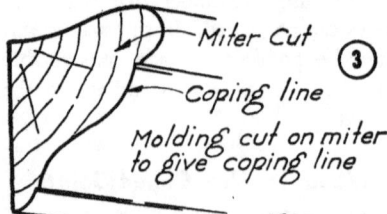

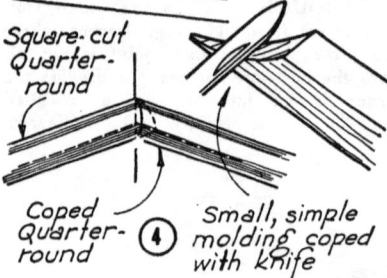

to fit over the other molding as shown in Fig. 2, will appear to fit reasonably well no matter how much the wood shrinks.

Amateurs often find it difficult to cope one molding to another, especially if it is at all complicated. That is only because they do not know the very simple trick used by carpenters to provide a cutting line. The molding which is to be coped is merely cut at a 45° angle in a miter box. The line formed by the intersection of the miter cut and the face of the molding, Fig. 3, is the line to follow with the saw. If this is accurately done, the coped molding will fit perfectly when butted against the molding.

Coping is usually done with a coping saw; in fact it was from this common operation that the saw got its name. In case of a small quarter-round molding or something almost as simple, it is often quicker and easier to whittle the end to shape with a sharp pocketknife as in Fig. 4.

were thicker than the rail, which is frequently the case. The bridle joint shown in Fig. 2 is therefore much better. As a rule the joint is laid out to leave one third the thickness of the wood in the horizontal member.

In making such a joint, allow sufficient stock on the vertical piece so that the slot

SMALL WAXED BLOCK PRESSES SAW FLAT AGAINST TOP OF RAIL WHILE SAWING OFF PROJECTIONS OF BRIDLE JOINT

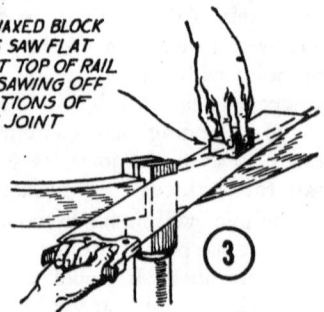

③

will be deeper than the width of the rail. After the joint has been glued, the projecting ends can be sawed off flush. A safe and accurate way to do this is shown in Fig. 3. Use a sharp, fine-set handsaw and hold the blade flat against the top of the rail with a small block of wood on which paraffin from a candle or other wax has been rubbed. If this trick is used in this

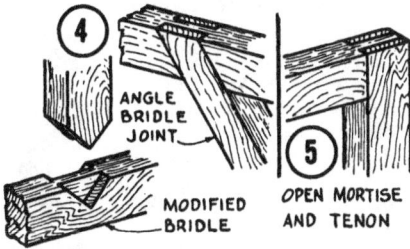

ANGLE BRIDLE JOINT

MODIFIED BRIDLE

OPEN MORTISE AND TENON

and other cases when it is necessary to cut off some projecting part, a cut can be made that is perfectly true. It can then very easily be dressed with a few strokes of a finely set block or smooth plane.

Bridle joints are also used in various types of heavy framing and are sometimes modified as in Fig. 4, which also shows an angle bridle. The open mortise-and-tenon joint is very similar to a bridle and may be confused with it, but it is usually an external joint at the corner of a frame as shown in Fig. 5.

The Fabulous Shiplock Joint

IF YOU read much about the ancient lore of woodworking, you are bound to come across occasional references to the shiplock joint. Not one woodworker out of a hundred today could even identify the joint,

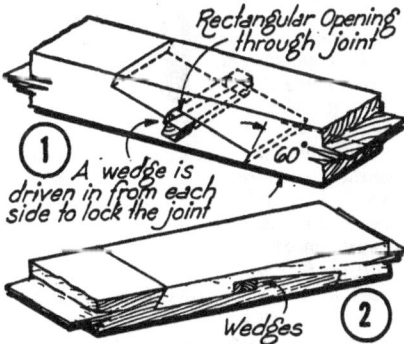

Rectangular Opening through joint

A wedge is driven in from each side to lock the joint

Wedges

yet it is always mentioned with wonderment and respect.

The shiplock is, indeed, a remarkable joint. It was used by old-time New England ship's carpenters for joining timbers end to end for keels and other heavy frame members. When there were no ships to build, these carpenters turned their attention to barns and houses and, naturally, introduced the same joint for sills, girts and plates. Even today when house wreckers come across timbers joined in this way, they either saw the wood or drag the timbers apart with a truck or tractor.

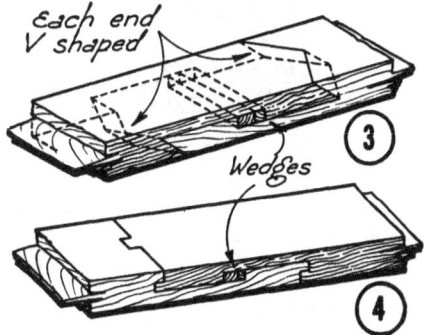

Each end V shaped

Wedges

For thick timbers, the joint was usually made as shown in Fig. 1. The formal name for this joint is a joggled and wedged splice or scarf. For thinner timbers, the variation shown in Fig. 2 was common.

A rarer version, which was called a scarf joint with V'd ends, is illustrated in Fig. 3. Another variation of this joint—and probably one of the best scarfed joints ever designed—is shown in Fig. 4, but it was relatively uncommon because of the work involved in making it. It is called the double-tenoned scarf joint.

Edges Beveled for Tight Fit

WHERE one board has to lap over the edge of another in a perfectly tight-fitting joint, better results can often be obtained if the edge is planed or jointed on a slight bevel. One of the most common applications of this idea is in making ordinary, full-size door frames. It is the practice of many carpenters to bevel the edges of the side jambs as shown. The trim or casing members can then be nailed on with assurance that the joint will be

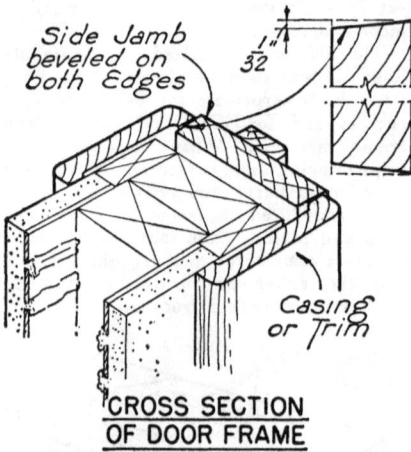

Side Jamb
beveled on
both Edges

$\frac{1}{32}$"

Casing
or Trim

CROSS SECTION
OF DOOR FRAME

other structural element in such a way as to prevent any possibility that it will spread or pull apart, the joint can be modified to a middle-lap dovetail, which is made as shown in Fig. 2. This joint withstands tension very well, requires no more stock to make and is not much more difficult to lay out and cut.

Taking Glued Joints Apart

EVERY home craftsman who attempts to repair furniture is certain to encounter the problem of taking apart glued joints. In many cases this is comparatively easy. The glue has given away or deteriorated, the wood of one member has shrunk or the joint has been so badly racked in use that it is quite loose.

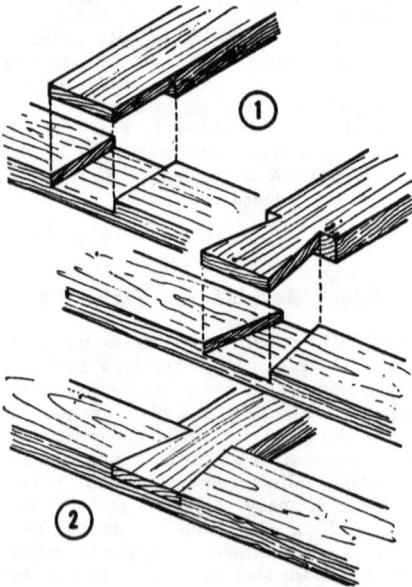

Sometimes, however, repair work requires the separation of joints which still hold stubbornly. This is often the case when certain joints in a chair or other piece of furniture have become loose, but others are still holding securely, yet some of the strong joints have to be taken apart in order to permit the weak ones to be reglued. Another case is when a member has been seriously damaged and has to be replaced, yet the joints at the ends still hold firmly.

If one or more joints in a piece of furniture are so loose that they can be opened sufficiently to insert a little glue, a passable repair can be made in most cases without disturbing the other nearby tight joints.

Wedge the joint open as far as possible, as shown in the sketch, but take great pains not to overstrain the good joints or damage any finished surfaces. A stick of wood can often be used to wedge members apart provided cardboard or cloth is used to protect the surface of the furniture from being scratched or dented. Bar clamps or hand screws can sometimes be used in reverse to push joints apart.

tight throughout its entire length. There is some advantage in doing this even when special molded trim is used which has the back slightly recessed to make easier the task of fitting it tight along the edges.

Dovetail Improves Lap Joint

THE so-called "middle-lap joint" shown in Fig. 1 is often used for fastening a bracing piece across a large, flat frame and for other similar purposes. When it is important to reinforce the frame or

When the tenon, dowels or other elements of the joint have been opened as far as is deemed safe, the old glue on the exposed surfaces may be carefully scraped

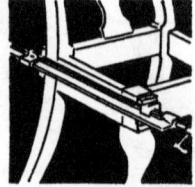

off or, in many cases, removed with warm water and a stiff bristle brush.

Fresh glue is now applied with a sliver of wood, bit of veneer or small brush. A high-grade glue should be used as the permanence of the repair depends entirely upon the strength of the glue. For such work, a glue of gap-filling qualities is desirable when the joint can no longer be regarded as being tight and well fitted. Of the glues commonly available for amateur use, a good casein glue, if used in a stiff mixture, and the comparatively new resorcinol-resin glue, which is also completely waterproof and heatproof, have marked gap-filling characteristics. On the other hand, the urea-resin glues, although excellent woodworking adhesives, are not gap-filling glues and should be used only for smooth, well-fitted joints.

The joint should then be forced together and held with clamps, weights, a tourniquet of rope or other means until the glue has had time to set. Be sure to remove the squeeze-out with a damp rag before it hardens.

If a joint is loose and weak, yet cannot be spread apart sufficiently to insert any glue, it is possible to force glue in by means of a special injector. This is a commercial tool which consists of two parts— a very fine drill for drilling one or more holes into the heart of the joint and a syringe, which resembles a large hypodermic syringe, with which the glue can be forced through the hole with enough pressure to cause it to flow through the joint cavity. The hole or holes are then patched with stick shellac or other suitable filler.

Suppose, however, there is no escape from taking apart joints that hold firmly. Start with the one that seems the least secure and endeavor to loosen it by the methods already described.

When this won't work out, the next method is the use of hot water or possibly steam to soften the glue. The main thing to consider here is the finish. If you intend to refinish the piece after it has been repaired, you need not worry about the effect of water and heat. This is true, too, if the finish is water and heat resistant. To test it, try the effect of a little boiling water on some hidden or inconspicuous part.

Provided it is safe to proceed, you can apply hot water on cloths around the joint. It may or may not work, depending upon how readily the moisture and heat can penetrate the joint and whether or not the wood swells so much that the joints remain tight even after the glue has been softened.

You have to take it for granted, of course, that the glue used was of a type which can be softened in this way. This is usually true. It is only certain types of modern factory-built furniture or furniture made by home craftsmen which is likely to have the joints glued with water-resistant and heatproof glues, and such joints rarely fail or require repairs.

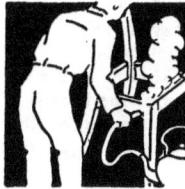

Steaming is the most drastic method and should be tried only as a last resort. It is the only way, however, to get some joints apart.

Suppose none of these methods will work. The solution then is to cut the joint. The cut is made alongside the joint with the finest, thinnest saw available. In small, delicate work, a coping saw, dovetail saw or hacksaw blade may be used.

If the member which is to be removed is damaged and requires to be replaced with new wood, it isn't necessary to be so careful. The cuts can be made an inch or two from the joints and the remaining stubs split with a chisel and pried or cut out. In the case of mortised joints, the mortises are cleaned out with a chisel and close-fitting hardwood blocks glued in to plug the openings. The new member, after being made and fitted, is fastened with dowels and glue or in any way that seems most suitable.

When joints have to be cut and the old member glued back in place, the same method is used, but the piece must be patched to compensate for the small amount of wood lost by the saw cuts.

PART 2
Fastening and Gluing

IF YOU drive a 1" No. 12 steel wood screw about three quarters of its length into the face of a cypress board, it will take a pull of about 230 pounds to draw it out. In hard maple, the force required to pull it out would be well over 800 pounds. This indicates the great holding power of wood screws.

In using wood screws, the first question to arise is the size of screw to select. The size of the screw is a combination of diameter and length as shown in Fig. 1.

Frequently the thickness of the boards or work limits the length of the screws that can be used as shown in Fig. 2. In that

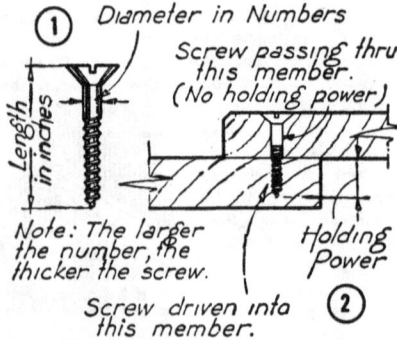

is to be used, then the screw must enter the second piece seven times $\frac{7}{16}$" which is $1\frac{7}{16}$". Since the screw must also pass through $\frac{3}{4}$" of the piece being fastened, the overall length of the screw should be $1\frac{7}{16}$" plus $\frac{3}{4}$" which equals $2\frac{3}{16}$". Since the closest screw to this length is 2", then a 2" No. 9 screw will give maximum holding power in this case.

If you have some choice as to the length of the screw, select a long screw of smaller diameter rather than a short screw of larger diameter. This may surprise you, but many tests by the U. S. Bureau of Standards have shown that a long slender screw will hold better than a short thick one.

Charts are available in many handbooks showing the size bit or drill to use for drilling clearance holes and lead holes as shown in Fig. 4 for any size screw. If the chart is as complete as it should be, you will notice that two figures are given for the lead holes—one showing the size to drill it in softwoods and the other in hardwoods. The lead hole in softwoods should be drilled about 70 percent as large as the core or root diameter of the screw, but in hardwoods the hole should be larger, or about 90 percent of the root diameter. You gain nothing by making the lead hole too small, but merely increase the risk of splitting the wood and the difficulty of driving the screws, especially in hard-

case, you have to decide only what diameter to select. Generally speaking, the thicker the screw, the greater its holding power when axially loaded. But this is true only up to a certain limit, after which the holding power is reduced as the diameter increases.

For maximum holding power a screw should enter the second piece of stock for a distance of seven times the diameter of the screw. Let's assume you are fastening two pieces together, driving the screw into edge grain as shown in Fig. 3. If a No. 9 screw

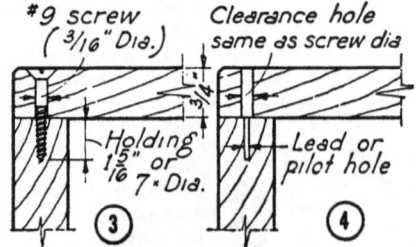

(5) Counterbored hole with plug

Button plug

(6) Phillips Head Screw

If a chart is not at hand, drill the clearance holes for the shank of the screw slightly larger than the diameter of the shank. Drill the lead hole for the remainder of the screw with a drill one half the diameter of the shank. In hardwoods, the lead hole should not be smaller than this or there will be some danger of splitting the wood or possibly breaking the screw.

Do not hesitate to use a hammer to start a screw into the lead hole. This will not weaken the joint provided the screw is driven only part way in with the hammer.

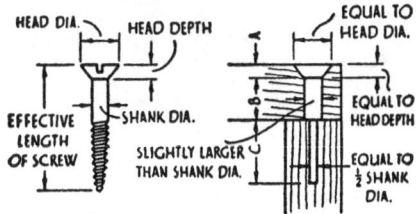

HEAD DIA. HEAD DEPTH EQUAL TO HEAD DIA.

EFFECTIVE LENGTH OF SCREW SHANK DIA. SLIGHTLY LARGER THAN SHANK DIA. EQUAL TO HEAD DEPTH EQUAL TO ½ SHANK DIA.

A – COUNTERSUNK SECTION OF HOLE IN FIRST MEMBER
B – CLEARANCE HOLE IN FIRST MEMBER
C – PILOT HOLE IN SECOND MEMBER

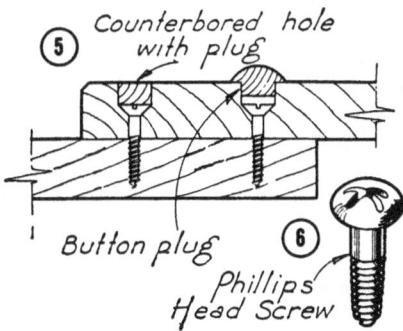

woods. The application of a lubricant such as soap will make screws easier to drive without any noticeable loss of holding power.

In fine work where the screw heads must be concealed as shown in Fig. 5, it is customary to counterbore the holes and, after the screws have been driven, glue in face-grain plugs made from the same kind of wood as the body of the work. For less particular work, screw-hole buttons or oval-top flush plugs are used. These are stocked by some craftwork supply houses and the larger hardware stores.

Another expedient is to use Phillips recessed-head wood screws shown in Fig. 6, the heads of which are generally regarded as less objectionable in appearance than ordinary slotted screw heads.

For delicate work, screws can be obtained in very small sizes. The smallest commercial wood screw, No. 0, is only about $\frac{1}{16}$" in body diameter. The very small sizes of brass and nickel-plated wood screws are stocked by craftwork supply houses and it pays to keep an assortment of them on hand. They can often be used to advantage in place of escutcheon pins.

Pilot Holes for Wood Screws

WHEN drilling holes to receive wood screws, the amateur woodworker will have better results and joints will be stronger if he refers to a chart for guidance as to exactly the right size drills to use. These charts are available in many handbooks.

At the same time, it has the advantage of giving the screw a good, straight start so that it can be driven more easily with the screw driver.

If the screw threads are scraped over a bar of beeswax or hard soap, the screw will go into hardwood with less effort.

In white pine and other very soft woods, a flathead screw can usually be sunk flush with the surface without countersinking the hole in advance. However, the work will look neater if the hole is countersunk. In hardwoods, countersinking is essential for flathead screws.

A good workman takes pains not to countersink the lead hole too deeply. To do this, stop countersinking before the hole has become too wide and test with the head of the screw which is to be used, as shown.

Tips on Working with Screws

WOOD screws have a tendency to work loose in time if the parts which they hold together are exposed to vibration or jarring. One of the best ways to prevent this is to notch the screw threads with a cold chisel as shown at A before driving them. Some mechanics merely flatten the sharp edges of the thread by laying the screw on a metal block and hammering it.

Steel screws are sometimes difficult to

33

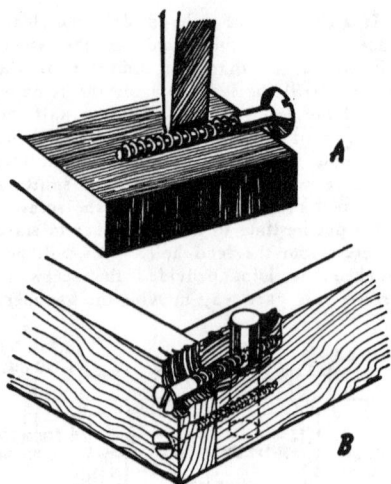

insert the screws that the heads will be damaged or broken. On the other hand, if oversize lead holes are drilled, the screws will not hold properly.

A common expedient is to drill the holes oversize and plug them with soft wood, but this does not guarantee any great degree of permanency. A better method is to drill the pilot holes the correct size (using a drill of one diameter for the threaded portion and a larger diameter for the shank of the screw). Then tap the smaller hole to receive the screw threads with a tap made from a screw of the same size as that which is to be used. This tap is made by filing away half the screw as shown. When turned into the hole, it will cut clean, accurate threads. After the tap screw has been removed, the regular screw can be driven easily into the threaded hole and will hold with full strength.

remove because they have become rusty. The time-honored method of loosening them is to apply a hot soldering iron to the head. The heat causes the metal to expand, and as it cools and contracts, the screw usually becomes loose enough to be withdrawn without danger of breaking the head.

When a screw will not hold in end-grain wood, or if the wood has cracked, it is possible as a rule to insert a dowel crosswise as shown at B. The screw will hold firmly in the hardwood dowel.

If Screws Are Hard to Drive

TO DRIVE wood screws in ivory, ebony and certain extremely hard, dense woods is often quite difficult. If ordinary pilot holes are drilled or bored into the material, so much force will be required to

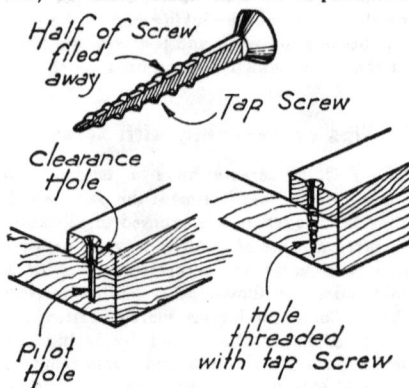

Hints on Using Brass Screws

BRASS wood screws are comparatively soft and therefore easily damaged while being driven. The screw driver is likely to slip and crush or distort the edges of the slot so that the blemish is conspicuous. This always gives the impression of careless workmanship.

To avoid having to use too much force in driving brass screws, be sure the lead holes are of the correct size and depth,

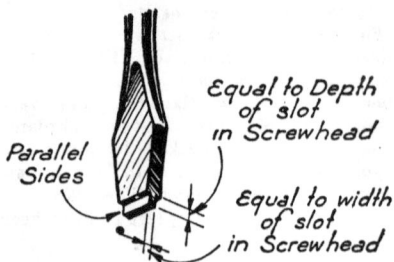

especially in hardwood. Rubbing the screw threads on a cake of beeswax or soap will also make them easier to drive.

It is essential to select a screw driver that fits the slot properly. Even so, the screw driver, as ordinarily ground, may slip. When a number of small brass screws are to be used, it pays to grind the point of the screw driver to the shape shown so that it will fit the slot snugly. This shape, with parallel sides, is less likely to slip than the standard tapered point and will leave the slots unmarred.

Substitute Oval-head Screws

FOR applying certain types of surface hardware · and for other work which requires a decorative appearance, it is sometimes desirable to use oval-headed rather than flathead or roundhead wood screws. The correct size of oval-headed screws may not be on hand and often cannot readily be obtained from a small local hardware store. In such cases it takes only a few minutes to reshape the heads of flathead

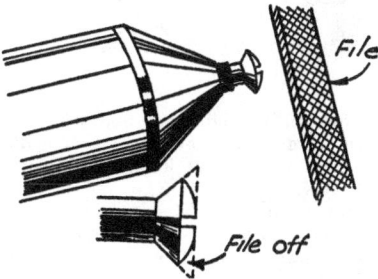

screws. Chuck the screws in a lathe or drill press and file them with a smooth-cut or other fine flat file and polish them with emery cloth. In the absence of power tools, clamp a hand drill in the vise and use it to revolve the screws while the heads are being filed. A good polish can then be given the heads with a piece of emery cloth.

Ways to Start Small Screws

ALL sorts of methods are used by mechanics to start tiny machine screws into tapped holes or place very small wood screws in position for driving. One old standby is to

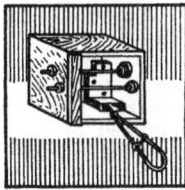

double a bit of friction tape over the end of the screw driver, using one or more thicknesses as necessary so that the blade will fit the slot of the screw so tightly that the screw will not fall off. Another, favored by some woodworkers, is to whittle the end of a small dowel or other hardwood stick to fit the slot of the screw so that it has to be forced in place. After the pilot hole has been drilled, the stick is used to insert the screw point and make the first one or two turns; then it is withdrawn and the screw driver substituted.

Anyone who prefers a less makeshift

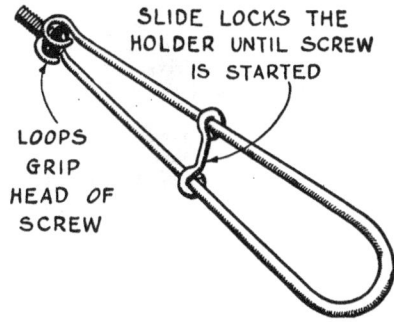

SLIDE LOCKS THE HOLDER UNTIL SCREW IS STARTED

LOOPS GRIP HEAD OF SCREW

method, however, can bend up a screw starter from soft wire as shown. It serves like tweezers to grip any size screw by the head, and the two loops are then locked by pulling back the crosspiece.

Cloth Starts Screws in Tight Places

A PIECE of cloth can be used to help start a screw in a hard-to-reach spot. The screw is first forced through the center of the cloth, the screwdriver blade is then placed in the slot of the screw and the cloth is twisted tightly around the blade and on up to the handle where it is gripped with the hand.

In this manner a screw can be started in a place that can be reached by a screwdriver while inaccessible to the hand. After the screw has been started, the cloth is unwound and torn free of the screw.

This same principle can be enlisted to grip a bolt or nut in an open-end wrench. The rag is placed over the head of the bolt, and the wrench is then forced over it.

Steel-Wool Plugs Hold Screws

THE next time you have to attach shelving, towel racks, cabinets, mirrors or other furniture or fittings to a brick, plaster or concrete wall and do not have on hand suita-

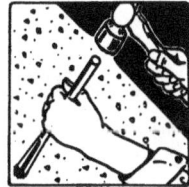

ble fiber plugs or expansion bolts, try this method:

After deciding on the size screws required to hold the fixture, drill somewhat larger holes into the masonry or plaster with a star drill or twist drill, depending on the hardness of the material. Plug these holes with medium fine steel wool and pack it in as firmly as possible, using a nail set or punch and hammer to compress it tightly. When the screws are driven into the hard-packed steel wool, they will hold surprisingly well.

Workbenches and power tools can be fastened to a concrete floor with lag screws by using this method and they will not be likely to work loose.

Cutting Short Machine Screws

WHEN it is necessary to cut or file a machine screw or stove bolt that is too short to be held in a vise without damaging the threads, a device made of hardwood can be used as shown in the sketch

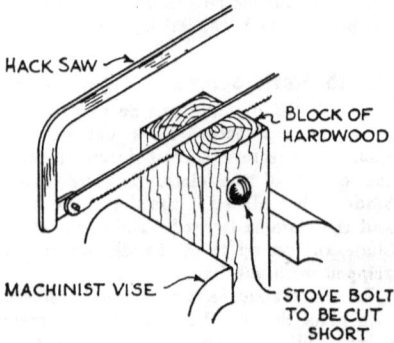

HACK SAW

BLOCK OF HARDWOOD

MACHINIST VISE

STOVE BOLT TO BE CUT SHORT

to hold the screw. The holder is nothing more than a piece of wood with a small hole bored in it, and the screw is turned into the hole. The point at which the hack saw is used to cut into the wood will depend on the length that is required for the screw. After the screw has been cut, the stock on the far side can be cut off, leaving the short length of the screw in the wood where the end may be filed smooth without difficulty.

Screws for Fastening Plaster

SOMETIMES a small section of plaster on an old ceiling—and less frequently on a wall—comes loose because the plaster keys which hold it to the wooden laths or plaster-board backing have broken off. If the plaster hasn't cracked and is otherwise in good condition, it can be fastened securely with a special type of screw which you can prepare yourself. Ordinary wood screws won't do because the heads are not large enough; and nails can't be driven in because the laths are so springy that

the vibration is almost certain to crack the plaster.

To make the screws, get a few 1¼" large-headed roofing nails—not the ordinary small-head type. Then cut a spiral groove in each as shown with a small rat-

Modified Roofing Nail

tail file while holding the nail with pliers or in a small vise or clamp. A shallow slot must also be cut in the head with a hack saw.

Drill small holes where the screws are to go and lubricate the threads with beeswax or hard soap. The screws can then be driven in the usual way, and their large heads will hold the plaster firmly in place. If the heads are sunk slightly into the plaster, they can be concealed with patching plaster, and the ceiling or wall painted or papered to conceal the repair.

This expedient, of course, is not suitable where the plaster has been laid on metal lath or where the plaster has become badly cracked. In some cases, however, it will save an expensive plastering job.

Technique of House Nailing

THE strength of any wood structure depends to an important extent on how well the parts and elements are fastened together. The principal fastenings in a wood-framed

house are nails, and its solidity is largely determined by the effectiveness of the nailing. In erecting wood buildings it is therefore important to know the size, number and placement of nails required to withstand the forces that the parts of a house must resist.

That nailing is a major factor in developing strong and rigid frame houses is shown by the action of storms. Many well-nailed and well-constructed wood buildings have survived for decades the severe weather cycles and the occasional storms of hurricane intensity that occur in many parts of the country. On the other hand, under severe storm conditions, houses with inadequate nailing often separate into parts or even into individual pieces of framing, few of which are actually broken. This demonstrates that the weakness was in the nailing rather than in the wood parts themselves.

The home craftsman who intends to construct a garage, an extension to his house or a summer cottage can avoid many mistakes in nailing if he obtains a copy of the new Government publication titled "Technique of House Nailing." This publication does not favor any particular design of framing, but merely refers to acceptable practice in assembling and arranging parts in any structurally well-designed frame house of the balloon, platform, or other type. It limits nailing instructions largely to structural details necessary for rigidity and strength without considering trim or other decorative parts.

A copy of the publication can be obtained from the Superintendent of Documents, U. S. Government Printing Office, Washington 25 D. C., at a cost of 20 cents. Payment should be made by postal note, money order or check.

Making Strong Nailed Joints

HOME craftsmen are well aware of the fact that ordinary nailed joints often appear to deteriorate in strength with age. Perhaps the most common and familiar examples are wooden floors and stairways, which are likely to develop squeaks here and there due to the fact that the nails are no longer holding the floor boards or pair members together.

In the presence of moisture, the weakening of nailed joints is still more marked. Recent tests have shown that the loss in axial holding power of ordinary nails may be as high as 71 percent in shingles and siding. In the case of flooring brads and cut nails it may be as high as 42 percent.

The modern method of overcoming this decline in strength is to use helically threaded nails such as those known as "Screwtite" nails*, or annularly threaded nails, such as "Stronghold" nails*. With these nails the resistance to withdrawal is increased as high as 70 percent has been observed.

* "Screwtite" and "Stronghold" nails, also "Stronghold Screwnails," are manufactured by the Independent Nail & Packing Company, Bridgewater, Mass.

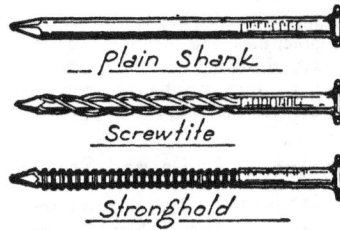

Plain Shank

Screwtite

Stronghold

While few amateurs know about these nails, their use has been increasing in industrial work. The Virginia Polytechnic Institute Wood Research Laboratory recently published a booklet on "Immediate vs. Delayed Holding Power of Nails".

"Summarizing these test results on straight and slant-driven nails," the report says, "the grand-average delayed withdrawal resistance was 32 percent smaller for plain-shank nails and 13 percent larger for threaded-shank Stronghold Screwnails than their immediate withdrawal resistance; while the grand-average delayed lateral load-carrying capacity was approximately 5 percent smaller than the immediate lateral load-carrying capacity for both types of nails."

How to Prevent Nail Spotting

SO-CALLED "nail spotting" sometimes causes trouble on walls covered with gypsum and other types of wallboard. The spots are more likely to appear on outside walls and on the ceilings of the upper floor.

The reason why dust collects in spots over the nails is because the surface of the wall over the nailheads is slightly colder than the remainder of the wallboard area. The difference in temperature accounts for the spots, as more dust collects on the colder areas of a wall.

The modern way to prevent spotting is to fasten the wallboard on exterior walls and top-floor ceilings with plastic-headed nails. The heads are long and cone shaped. The area over these nailheads is so nearly the same temperature as the remainder of the wallboard that spotting is minimized.

It is also possible to obtain so-called "predecorated nails" for use in fastening wallboard where the nails are not to be concealed by plaster or battens. These are fourpenny nails with heads colored to match knotty pine, bleached mahogany or walnut. They are designed especially for wood-grained gypsum wallboard, but can be used wherever the colors are appropriate.

Rustproof Nails and Screws

IN ASSEMBLING outdoor furniture, trellises or any work which is likely to be exposed to dampness, it is desirable to use rustproof nails, screws and bolts. Brass screws, however, are expensive, and galvanized screws and nails, as well as copper nails, are not always readily available in the sizes desired. It therefore becomes necessary to use ordinary wire nails and bright steel screws and bolts. These will give longer service if they are coated with rosin to render them moisture resistant.

The method is very simple. The nails or screws are heated slightly in a pan, then dipped into another pan full of powdered rosin and shaken around. This gives them a thin protective coating of rosin.

Prevent Bolts from Rusting

BY DIPPING threads of a bolt in shellac before screwing on a nut, trouble will be prevented where rust may cause them to stick together. The shellac will cover the surface and stop rust from forming.

Graphite on Screws Prevents Rust

SCREWS made of steel are apt to rust if exposed to the weather. One method of preventing rust is to coat the screw with a mixture of graphite and soft tallow before driving it.

When to Sand Before Gluing

THE difficulties which amateurs sometimes experience in obtaining durable glued joints may be due to the nature of the woods being glued rather than poor glue or improper gluing methods. For example, if a wood contains oil or pitch, as do certain pines and other commonly used woods, a film is likely to form on the surface and this may interfere with effective gluing, especially if a urea or plastic resin glue is used.

The remedy is a simple one—just sandpaper the surfaces or edges to be glued. If the sanding is done within a day of the gluing operation, the glue will take hold

better. On the other hand, if the surfaces are sanded a long time before the gluing operation, which often is the case when an amateur works on a project for several weeks before the final assembly, the pitch and oil will have time to ooze out and form a new film. When in doubt, therefore, sand before gluing with urea resin glue.

With casein glue, this precaution doesn't seem necessary for the reason that casein glue is alkaline and therefore penetrates the surface film just as any alkaline cleaner.

Some woods, such as teak, yew, osage orange, pitch pine and lemonwood, are so oily that sanding alone may not be sufficient to insure strong, permanent glued joints with urea resin and other neutral or slightly acid glues.

In addition to oily woods, any specially hard, dense, smooth materials such as Micarta and Formica, should be sanded before glue is applied.

Extra Strong Glued Joints

SOME woods, especially those of an oily nature such as teak, lemonwood and pitch pine, or woods which are exceedingly hard and dense, like rock maple, are much more difficult to glue than others. To insure very strong joints, some woodworkers brush the edges to be joined with a ten percent solution of caustic soda. If caustic soda is not available, a household cleaning compound will usually give the same results.

The soda or cleaning compound is allowed to remain for about ten minutes, when the excess is wiped off. After the surfaces are dry, the joints are glued in the usual way with casein or hide glue (not a urea resin or other glue which might be affected by any trace of alkali).

In the case of a wood such as osage orange, which is especially difficult to glue, the caustic soda treatment may increase the shearing strength of the joint from 300 or 400 to 3,000 pounds.

Those who do much gluing with difficult woods, such as archery enthusiasts, nowadays save themselves the trouble of pretreating the joints by using the comparatively new resorcin resin glue. It gives strong joints without taking any special precautions. However, in the case of very oily woods like osage orange, it is desirable to heat the work moderately while the glue is setting. One or more common infrared heat lamps form a convenient source of heat for this and other gluing operations.

How to Avoid Glue Stains

SOME craftsmen are partial to casein glue because they have used it for years and have found it a satisfactory heavy-duty adhesive which they can depend upon for strength even on rough work and comparatively loose-fitting joints. However, they sometimes run into difficulties because all ordinary casein glues will stain certain woods, especially those, like chestnut and oak, which contain a considerable amount of tannin.

The best preventive is to apply the glue with special care, using only enough to give a good joint so there will be hardly any squeeze-out. This is somewhat difficult to do, with an ordinary glue brush, but is possible if a small, flat brush is used and all drips and runs are avoided. If the glue can be applied by means of a glue roller mounted on the glue container, it is much easier to spread a uniform coat that will not run over the edges.

The best remedy, if stains do appear, is to remove them with a bleach. A saturated solution of oxalic acid applied with a fiber brush is usually adequate for this purpose. When the bleach is partly dry, the acid should be neutralized with a strong, hot solution of borax. After the areas are completely dry, they may be sanded, and if necessary, the bleaching can be repeated.

In most cases it is simpler to keep on hand some nonstaining type of glue for work where staining may prove a problem, as in gluing up furniture which is to have a natural finish, veneering, and the more delicate forms of cabinetwork.

Preventing Dark Glue Stains

WHEN stock has been glued up for a table top or wide panels, it is a common sight to see a dark line running the length of the wood, caused by the dark glue that was used in joining the pieces. It is very difficult to remove this stain, with the result that it will show through the finish, especially if a light stain is used. If you use a dark glue, it is much simpler to prevent glue lines from showing rather than trying to remove them after they are in. With the aid of ordinary white chalk, all the trouble may be saved. Before the work is glued up, run the chalk along the *corners* of the edges that are to be joined. In this manner the chalk dust is worked into the grain and prevents the glue from penetrating at this point. Care should be taken not to get the chalk on the edges; otherwise the glue will not hold.

How to Make Glues Set Faster

IMPATIENCE spoils many glue joints. Amateur craftsmen are often in such a hurry to continue work on a project that they will not leave wood and veneers in the clamps or press for a sufficient length of time to allow the glue to set properly.

If you must hurry the work along, be sure to follow whatever instructions the glue manufacturer has provided for speeding the set of his product.

For example, if you are using one of the popular urea-resin powdered glues such as Cascamite, Weldwood or LePage's plastic resin glue, the setting period can be reduced by applying moderate heat to the joints. By far the most convenient way to do this is with an infrared heat lamp. As such lamps are now in common use in many homes, it is often possible to borrow one temporarily for the workshop. Since they are comparatively inexpensive, it is worth while to buy one if much gluing is being done with urea-resin glues. In the absence of such a lamp, place the work close to a radiator, hot air register, electric heater or other source of moderate heat.

It is very important, too, not to use these or certain other modern glues if the temperature of your shop or workroom is below 70° F. The wood, too, should be at least that warm. Don't take wood out of a cold lumber rack and glue it before it reaches room temperature.

The entirely waterproof resorcinol-resin glues such as Cascophen will set faster if the joints are exposed to heat, and they also should not be applied when the room temperature is under 70°.

Casein glues, which maintain considerable popularity because of their heavy-duty characteristics and their ability to hold on rough surfaces and in comparatively poorly fitted joints, can be used at much lower temperatures. With casein, you don't have to worry about how cold your workshop happens to be.

To make casein glues such as Casco or LePage's casein glue set more quickly, there is a trick with which few home craftsmen are familiar. Mix the glue with only half the usual amount of cold water so that it becomes a very thick paste. Let it stand for at least a quarter of an hour.

Then add slowly about half as much denatured alcohol as the original quantity of water. Acetone may be used instead of alcohol if available. This thins the glue to working consistency and makes it set quickly.

With high-grade liquid fish glues such as LePage's liquid glue, heat may be used to increase the speed of setting and is, in fact, the best way, as the addition of chemicals may affect the quality of the glue.

With glues such as Franklin liquid hide glue, heat may be used advantageously under certain conditions, but for a different purpose. If the glue is so cold that it does not spread readily, a moderate application of heat will bring it to normal consistency.

The comparatively new liquid polyvinyl-resin glues, which are white, are very fast setting. Even the most impatient craftsman cannot complain at the speed with which they harden. The only use for heat in their case is to keep a spread of glue soft if there is some unexpected delay in assembly. For example, if a piece of veneer on some small piece of craftwork slips after being glued and cannot be adjusted because the glue has already begun to take hold, a moderately hot iron pressed over the veneer will soften the glue sufficiently to allow the piece to be shifted.

To sum up, heat may be used to advantage to hasten the setting of three types of glue in common use—urea resin, liquid fish glue and resorcinol resin.

Gluing Tiles to a Wood Base

CERAMIC tiles are being used increasingly in amateur craftwork to make attractive tops for coffee tables, cocktail tables and garden tables and for serving trays, as well as for setting into flower boxes, plant stands, chests and various other types of furniture. Tiles suitable for this purpose may be purchased singly and in matched sets of four from some craftwork supply houses.

In many cases, as in the construction of trays or table tops, the tiles are cemented down on a plywood base. As an adhesive for this purpose, some experts recommend a thick mix of casein glue—about 1¼ measures of the casein powder to 1 measure of water. This is sometimes thickened with fine sawdust, especially if the surface on which the tiles are to be laid is somewhat rough and irregular or if the tiles themselves are ribbed, uneven or, as may be the case with homemade tiles, slightly warped. Made into a heavy paste with sawdust, the casein glue can be spread in a layer sufficiently thick to form a bed for the tiles, which should be pressed firmly in place and held down with weights until the glue hardens.

Still more convenient is one of the newer types of rubber-based industrial adhesives. These are very thick, tenacious cements that require little pressure and withstand moisture well.

To withstand extreme conditions of moisture and for outdoor use, it is better to fasten the tiles with a completely waterproof adhesive such as resorcinol-resin glue. If its dark color is objectional in the joints between the tiles, apply it only to the backs and then fill the face joints with any available white cement. A mixture of equal parts of urea-resin glue, very fine sawdust and ordinary white flour forms a good water-resistant crack filler for this and similar purposes, although it should not be used as an adhesive for cementing the tiles to their base.

Sometimes tiles may be encountered which have been made in such a way that even the backs are highly nonabsorbent. These are difficult or impossible to attach to a wooden surface with any woodworking glue. You can test porosity yourself by placing a few drops of water on the back of one of the tiles. If water is absorbed as it is when placed on unfinished wood, the tile can safely be glued by the methods previously mentioned. If, however, the water stays on the surface and is not absorbed, the safest thing to do is to use one of the special cements made for gluing nonporous and porous materials together.

An Adhesive for Unusual Uses

IF YOU do not have on hand a glue or cement that will stick glass to glass, leather to metal or other unusual combinations, burn some shellac in a dish to get rid of the alcohol. The sticky residue will serve in an emergency as a strong special-purpose glue.

A Cement for Sanding Disks

FASTENING a coated abrasive to a sanding disk can be quite a problem if the proper cement is not available. An excellent adhesive for this purpose can be prepared by the home craftsman. It requires the melting and mixing of 4 oz. of beeswax, 1 oz. of powdered rosin and 5 oz. of paraffin. This mixture should be melted and mixed in a double boiler rather than directly over an open flame.

After the material has been thoroughly mixed, it is poured in molds made of wood or cardboard having a cross section of about 1″ square. After the mixture has cooled, it is cut into blocks for ease in handling.

To use the cement, a block is pressed against the revolving disk and it is moved back and forth across the face until an even coat of the cement has been applied. The machine should then be stopped and the coated abrasive pressed against the cement-coated disk. Hand pressure is all that is necessary for this part of the operation. As soon as the coated abrasive has been applied, the disk is ready for use.

With the use of this cement, the coated abrasive adheres exceptionally well to the disk, although when necessary the abrasive may be pulled free from the disk without the slightest difficulty.

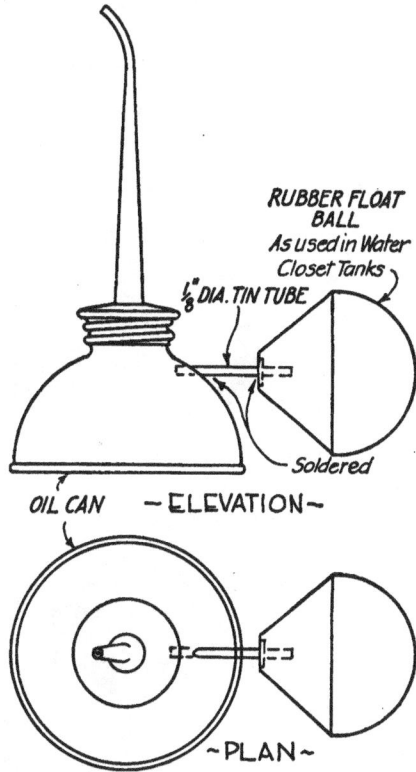

Oil-Can Gluer for Grooved Joints

ANY worker in wood knows it is difficult to get glue into a grooved joint without smearing glue on the surface of the wood. With an ordinary oil can, a metal tube and a rubber ball float from a flush tank, a gluer can be made. The tube is soldered to the oil can; then the brass bushing of the rubber float is drilled to take the other end of the tube. After the tube has been placed in the bushing, it is soldered to it. The glue is put in the oil

can and forced out by pressing on the float ball. The ball comes back to shape when pressure is released.

The glue applicator can be used for gluing plowed or grooved joints when building drawers or panels, for repairing furniture and toys and especially for applying glue in dowel holes.

Ways to Fasten Table Tops

TABLE tops, desk tops, cabinet tops and the like may be fastened in many ways. Only in the crudest type of construction are they attached to the supporting framework with unconcealed nails or screws driven from above, so numerous methods have been devised to attach them from underneath.

If a top is made of solid wood, it is obviously desirable to fasten it in such a way that it may expand and contract with atmospheric changes. When plywood is used for a top, the shrinkage and expansion is so slight that it may be disregarded.

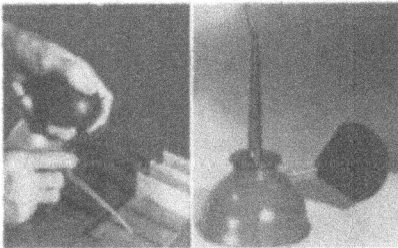

Offset

"A"

$\frac{1}{16}$" More than Offset

"B"

Clearance for expansion of Top

Top

"A"

$\frac{3}{8}$"

$\frac{3}{8}$"

$\frac{1}{2}$"

"B"

Rail

$\frac{3}{4}$" $\frac{3}{4}$" $2\frac{1}{2}$"

must, of course, be cut to suit, and it is important to locate them so that there is about ⅛" clearance between the button and the top before the screw is tightened. This is illustrated at B, Fig. 2.

Another type of metal fastener, often used in commercial work, is the so-called "figure 8." It is set into a shallow hole bored in the top of the rail and fastened with a screw as shown in Fig. 3. Another screw passes up into the table top. This type of fastener, although cheap and easy to install, doesn't allow the top to expand and contract as do the types shown in Figs. 1 and 2. Three-hole mending plates or their equivalent may be substituted for figure-8 fasteners as indicated in Fig. 4.

Amateurs sometimes favor the method

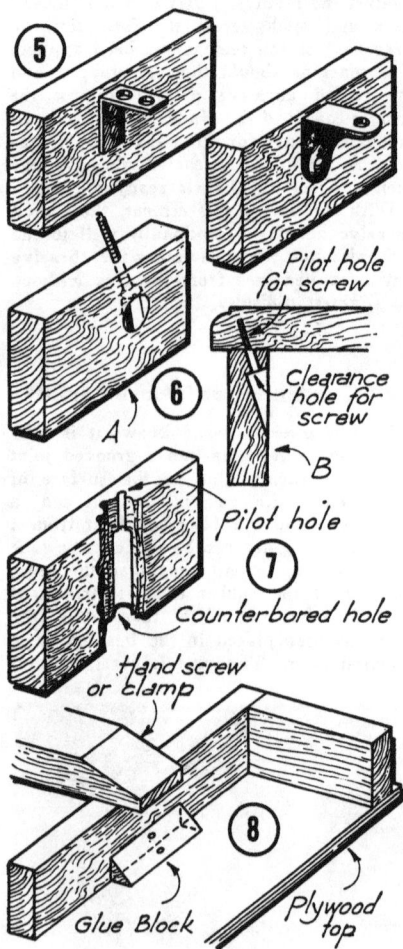

Pilot hole for screw

A

Clearance hole for screw

B

Pilot hole

Counterbored hole

Hand screw or clamp

Glue Block

Plywood top

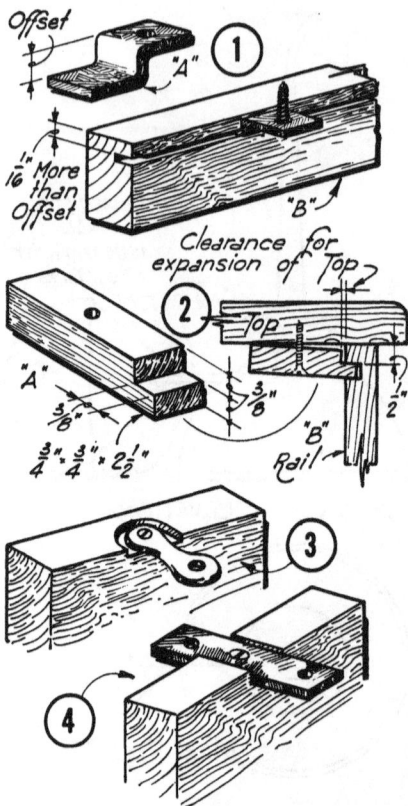

One of the most popular and best methods is to use offset table fasteners of the type shown at A, Fig. 1. These are sold by craftwork supply houses and the larger hardware stores. The width of the fasteners is usually ¾" and the offset ⅜", but it is advisable to buy the fasteners in advance so that the necessary slots can be cut on the bench saw in the table rails or other members as indicated at B, Fig. 1. In laying out the slots, add about 1/16" to the offset measurement so that the fasteners will draw the table top close against the rails when the screws are driven. As many fasteners as necessary may be used as they are very cheap and require only one screw apiece to install, once the slots have been cut.

If metal fasteners of this type are not on hand, wooden buttons may be made as shown at A, Fig. 2, from any available scraps of hardwood. The dimensions may be varied within reason. These buttons are used in the same way as the offset metal fasteners. The slots or gains in the rails

shown in Fig. 5, although it does not have too much to recommend it. Ordinary angle irons or corner braces are used. The former require four screws each, and the latter are more expensive although they require only two screws each and are very strong.

Provided the top of the table, desk or other piece of furniture overhangs the rails, it can be fastened with screws from below as shown at A, Fig. 6. The recess for starting the screws at an angle is bored into the inside face of the rail with an auger bit at least ½" in diameter. The bit is started straight in until the threads begin to take hold, then is slanted at an angle of about 60° so that the hole appears in cross section about as shown at B, Fig. 6. A clearance hole for the shank of the screw is then drilled with a bit of suitable size. If the top is of hard wood, a small pilot hole also has to be drilled in it.

Still another way to use screws alone for fastening a top is to counterbore holes through the rails as shown in Fig. 7 to within ¾" or 1" of the other edge, and drill clearance holes for the shanks of the screws the remainder of the distance. Since it is somewhat awkward to drive screws into deep counterbored holes, this method is better for work in which the rails are comparatively narrow.

Small plywood tops may be attached with triangular glue blocks tacked in with small nails or brads until the glue is hard. This method is illustrated in Fig. 8. Note that hand screws or clamps must be used to hold the top in place when this and certain other types of fastenings, such as that illustrated in Fig. 6, are employed. In fact, it is always a good idea to clamp two members together when practicable while fastening them permanently.

Screws may be used in a variation of the methods shown in Fig. 2. Plain blocks are prepared and fastened to the rails and the top as shown in Fig. 9. Note that the blocks should be placed about ⅛" below the top edge of the rails.

Finally, there are several ways of fastening a top down from above. If the top is of plywood or is relatively small and thick so that the expansion and contraction will not cause trouble, the parts may be clamped together and holes bored for dowels as shown in Fig. 10. The dowels are cut off flush with the top and allowed frankly to show, as in some very modern furniture and also certain types of early Colonial reproductions.

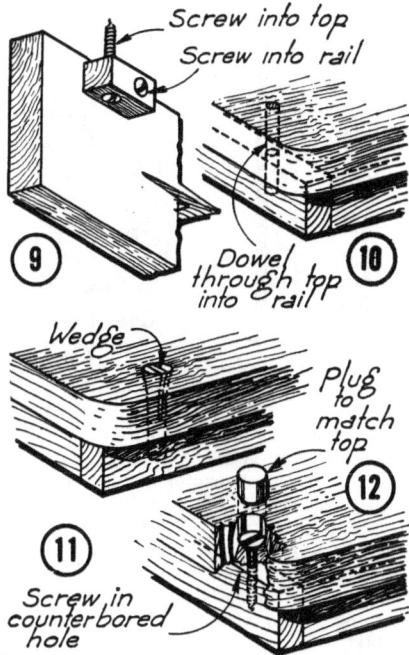

For greater strength, the dowels may be slotted for about 1" so that wedges can be driven in as indicated in Fig. 11. The slots are always placed across the grain of the top when of solid wood to prevent the great pressure from splitting the board. In plywood this is not important, but a crosswise wedge is more acceptable in appearance.

If screws are used, they may be inserted in counterbored holes, as in Fig. 12, and the holes plugged. If the plugs are cut from scraps of wood left over from the top so that they match perfectly, and are made in such a way that they show the face grain rather than end grain, they will be quite inconspicuous.

Two Ways to Fasten Bed Rails

WHEN an extra bed is needed for a guest room or for a child who has outgrown his crib, it is very easy for any handy man to make one because modern styles are so simple. All he has to do is look around in a furniture store and choose a design which he can adapt to his own purposes and build in a size to hold a standard spring and mattress.

Bed rails for a standard length spring should be 76" long. The head and foot

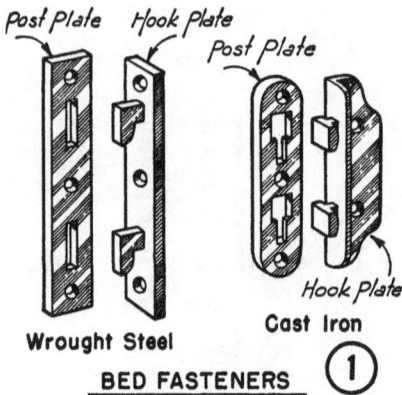

Post Plate Hook Plate Post Plate Hook Plate

Wrought Steel **Cast Iron**

BED FASTENERS ①

boards should be of such a size as to allow sufficient space between the bed rails to take the standard widths of springs. A full-size spring is 54″ in width and will require a space of 54½″ between the bed rails. A so-called three-quarter bed takes a spring 48″ wide and requires a space of 48½″ between the rails. A twin bed spring measures 39″ in width and requires a space of 39½″.

About the only construction problem involved is in fastening the side bed rails to the head and foot of the bed in such a way as to insure sufficient strength, yet permit the bed to be taken apart readily so that it can be moved whenever necessary.

The standard method is to use bed fasteners such as are shown in Fig. 1. These can be obtained from craftwork supply houses and some of the larger hardware stores. They come in sets of four

post plates and four hook plates. Standard sizes are 5″ and 6″ long.

If, for any reason, bed fasteners cannot be used—as, for example, when the rails are too narrow—the older method of mortising the rails into the posts may be followed as shown in Fig. 2. One long bolt ½″ or ⅝″ in diameter is used to hold each joint together.

When this method was in common use, the counterbored bolt holes in the posts were ordinarily concealed with what were known as brass bed-bolt covers like the one

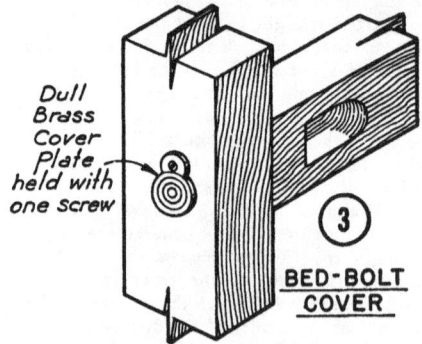

Dull Brass Cover Plate held with one screw

BED-BOLT COVER ③

sketched in Fig. 3. As these are not now easy to obtain, the home craftsman may use molded wood rosettes, also obtainable from craftwork supply houses, or make suitable plates along any style desired.

Substitute Bed-Rail Hangers

THE craftsman, constructing a bed, is often faced with the difficulty of obtaining hangers or fasteners by means of which the bed rail is attached to the posts. The sketches show how materials that can be obtained in any locality can be used to overcome this problem.

The basic materials required are a length of angle iron 1″ x 1″ x 3/16″, a length of 3/16″ x 1¼″ steel, and suitable nuts and bolts. The angle iron is cut into four lengths, each of which should be at least 4″ long. If the bed rails in question are wider than 5″, it is advisable to cut each length of angle longer than 4″. The flat steel should be cut into four lengths of 5″ each.

As shown in the drawing, two holes ⅜″ in diameter should be centrally located and drilled in each flat piece to take ⅜″ x ¾″ bolts or machine screws. Holes to correspond to these should be located

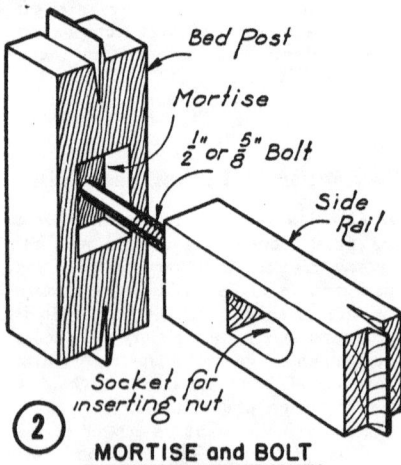

Bed Post

Mortise

½″ or ⅝″ Bolt

Side Rail

Socket for inserting nut

MORTISE and BOLT ②

CAP NUT TO BE
APPLIED AFTER
PASSING 1/4" BOLTS
THRU POST

RECESS TO
TAKE PLATE

BED
POST

HOLE TO
TAKE 1/4"
STOVE BOLT

STOVE BOLT TO
PASS THRU POST

3/8" x 3/4" BOLTS

3/16" PLATE

SHALLOW
HOLES TO
TAKE HEAD
OF 3/8" BOLTS

7/8" #8 F.H.
SCREWS

NUT TO
FIT 3/8" BOLT

1"x1"x3/16"
ANGLE

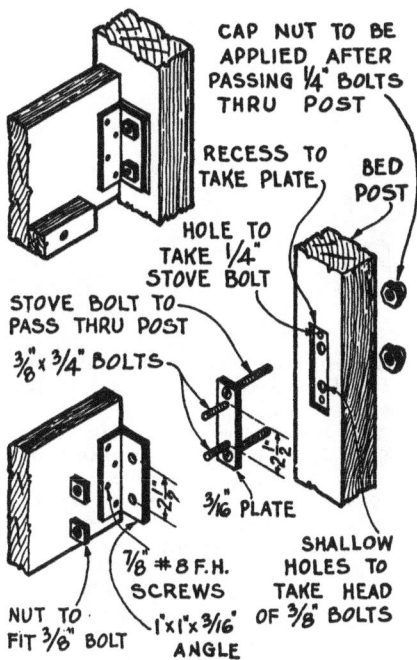

and drilled in one flange of the angle stock. The two holes that are to take the 1/4" stove bolts by means of which the flat plate is to be secured to the posts are located and drilled 3/8" from each end. These holes are countersunk on one side to take the flat head. The angle strip is to be secured to the bed rail by means of four flathead wood screws. At least four should be used. Holes to take these screws are drilled and countersunk.

Installing the hangers will require the attaching of the angle to the bed rail. The location of the bed rail should be established on the posts, then the flat steel plate placed on the post in its proper position. Using a knife, outline the position of the plate on the post. The plate can now be removed and the recess cut to take it. The plate is placed in the recess temporarily, so that the holes through the post that are to take the stove bolts, as well as the shallow holes that are to take the heads of the 3/8" machine screws, can be spotted. The plate is removed and the necessary holes are bored in the wood.

The 3/8" bolts are passed through the plate; then the plate is set in the recess. The stove bolts are inserted and a cap nut is applied to the end of each that is projecting beyond the opposite side of the post. If the bolt is too long to permit tightening the cap nut, the excess should be cut off with a hack saw so that it projects beyond the post no more than 3/16".

PART 3
Methods and Short Cuts

THE average home craftsman finds plywood one of his most useful materials in the construction of workshop projects. Not only is it readily available in large sizes, thus saving him considerable work in edge-gluing narrow boards, but plywood with fancy veneered faces is less expensive than solid stock. The biggest problem in using plywood for craft projects is how to conceal the edge of the plywood panels.

There are occasions when no amount of thought in designing corner joints can eliminate the use of plywood edge grain. In these cases some method of covering must be devised in order to hide the edge.

In an article of modern design, one of the most popular means of hiding the edge surface of plywood panels is by

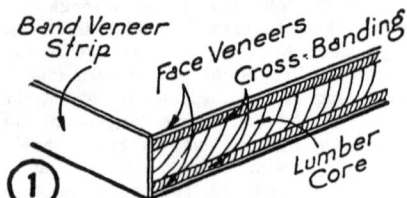

(1) 5-Ply Panel with banded veneer strip to hide edge grain

Band Veneer Strip — Face Veneers — Cross-Banding — Lumber Core

(2) Banding Rabbeted to face Veneer

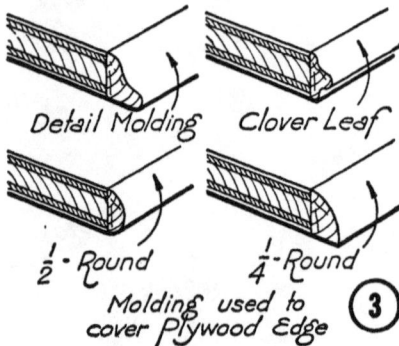

Detail Molding   Clover Leaf

½-Round   ¼-Round

(3) Molding used to cover Plywood Edge

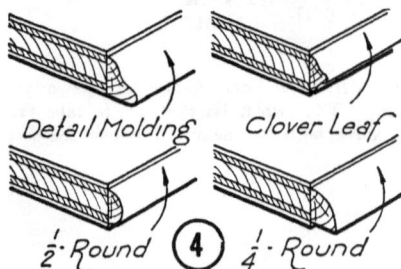

Detail Molding   Clover Leaf

½-Round (4) ¼-Round

One or more Face Veneers Left Exposed

(5) Edge Banding set in groove cut in lumber core of 5 ply panel

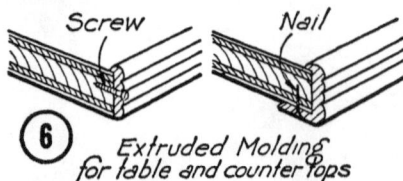

Screw   Nail

(6) Extruded Molding for table and counter tops

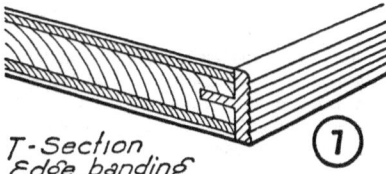

T-Section Edge banding

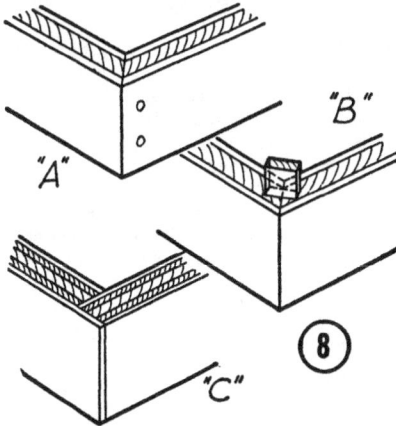

"A" "B" "C"

tive where half or quarter-round banding is used because of the more detailed effect which is obtained.

A novel edge treatment for plywood which is not often seen is shown in Fig. 5, while Fig. 6 shows the use of plastic or metal extruded edging. Most extruded trim is fastened to the plywood edge with brads or screws; however, one type, Fig. 7, is T-shaped and is held in place by forcing the tongue into a slightly under-sized groove.

The problem of unsightly edges can be solved, when practicable, by the use of a miter joint as shown at A, Fig. 8. This type of joint may be reënforced with glue blocks for greater strength when the design permits. To obtain a stronger joint and facilitate assembly, many craftsmen prefer to make the miter joint with a spline as at B, Fig. 8. For maximum strength, the grain direction of the spline should be at right angles to the joint.

Another popular method used where panels are joined at corners is shown at C, Fig. 8. In this type of construction one five-ply panel is rabbeted to the face veneer to receive the other panel. This is more easily machined than the miter joint, which when made across the face

banding them with the same type of wood used in the face veneer, as shown in Fig. 1. This is often used on shelf edges. The grain direction of the banding may be either lengthwise or crosswise, depending upon the desired effect.

For extra fine cabinetwork, this banding should be put on after undercutting the face veneer slightly to receive the banding strip, Fig. 2. This is often used on table and chests tops where it is desired to avoid any visible glue joint on the face surface. This type of joint requires the use of a very fine-toothed saw blade and an accurate setup on the circular saw so that the face veneer is not cut and spoiled. Quite satisfactory results, however, can be obtained by banding as illustrated in Fig. 1 and this type of construction is much simpler to manage.

Where a more ornamental or detailed edge is desired, a molded edge strip of a suitable design may be fastened to the plywood edge. Figure 3 shows several types of molding edging strips commonly used. The edging may be glued and bradded on, but for the best work the molding is attached with a spline and good quality glue.

Variations can be had by using a molding of a narrow width so that the edge of the plywood is not completely covered, Fig. 4. This treatment is especially effec-

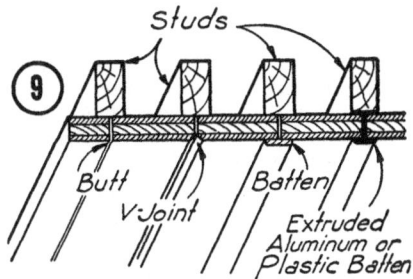

Studs

Butt V-Joint Batten Extruded Aluminum or Plastic Batten

Commonly Used Panel Joints

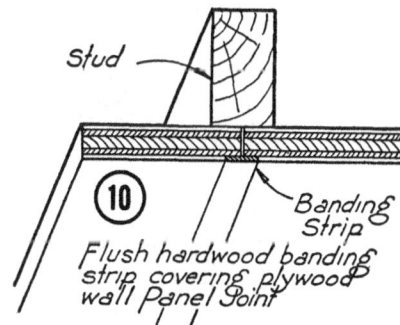

Stud

Banding Strip

Flush hardwood banding strip covering plywood wall Panel Joint

grain often results in a chipping out of the face veneer at the feathered edge. In making a miter joint the circular saw blade should be sharp and true in order to avoid tearing out the face veneer. For best results a hollow-ground blade should be used as the smooth edge it leaves can be glued without sanding.

Where plywood panels are used as wall covering, several different methods of jointing are possible, Fig. 9. If a hardwood veneer is used for paneling a room, a very effective method of covering panel joints is shown in Fig. 10. The flush banding strip which is glued to the rabbeted panel joint may be parallel to the face veneer, or a cross-grain strip of contrasting veneer may be used. An effective application of a cross-grain banding strip

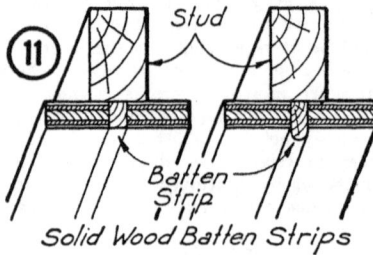

Solid Wood Batten Strips

is the use of walnut panel veneers with maple or birch batten veneers. Still another method of accomplishing the same effect is the use of a solid wood bead between panels as in Fig. 11.

Where plywood is used for bookshelves or in cabinets which are to be stained or painted, it is possible to shape the edge of the plywood with a detail cutter on the shaper, Fig. 12. This edge-shaped detail can be used where the article being made is to receive a dark stained finish. It is not well suited to light natural finishes because of the difficulty in equalizing

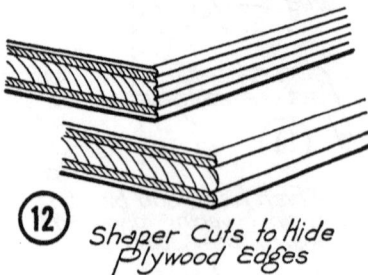

Shaper Cuts to Hide Plywood Edges

the stain between the end and edge grain of the plywood.

By experimenting with the many methods available, the home craftsman can usually find a method of edging plywood panels which will enhance the beauty of the project under construction.

Fitting Panel in Tight Groove

THERE are times when variations in the thickness of a plywood panel being inserted in a plowed rail or stile tend to split the dadoed member. In addition, the installing of such panel is quite difficult. Two methods of overcoming this problem are illustrated.

In Fig. 1 the cut may be made on the circular saw by running the panel between the rip fence and the saw blade to produce

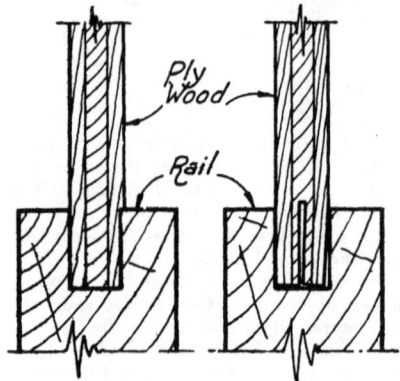

FIG. 1   FIG. 2

a rabbet and thus leave a tongue having the same thickness as the width of the dado or groove. If both sides of the panel will show when installed, care should be exercised so as not to make this cut too deep, which would cause an unsightly break.

The method shown in Fig. 2 also requires the use of the circular saw. The depth of the cut or saw kerf should be slightly greater than the depth of the dado or groove for which it is intended. The kerf cut should be made in the center of the plywood. While this is a better-appearing job than that obtained by the first method, it has the disadvantage of being weaker. If the panel is to be subjected to strain, preference should be given to the method shown in Fig. 1.

How to Make Rounded Corners for Modern Furniture

The Quarter-Round Sections Joining Top and Sides on Modern Pieces Are Made Semicircular and Split

MANY pieces of modern furniture call for rounded corners. Corners having a radius no greater than $\frac{3}{4}''$ are simple to make, but in most cases the radius is anything from $1\frac{1}{4}''$ to $2\frac{1}{2}''$, making it necessary to build up the corner from a block of wood and cut it to the required shape. Difficulty is never encountered when making the outside curve, but the cutting of the inner cove is a problem requiring explanation.

There are three methods by which a cove cut of this type may be made. Each in itself will prove satisfactory, but, two methods as seen in the sketches, require special tools, while the other one may be done by anyone owning a circular saw.

The quickest and easiest method of cutting a cove is on the spindle shaper. The average run of three blade cutters

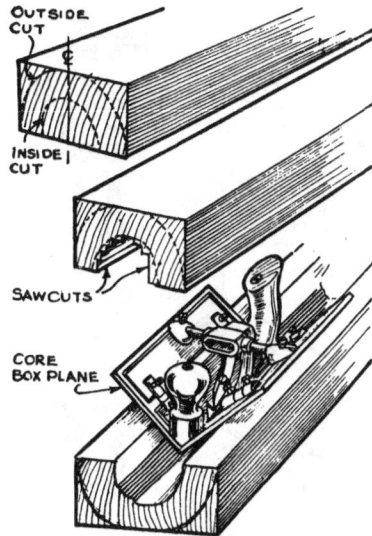

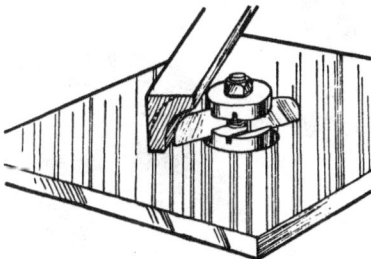

normally used on the shaper are satisfactory up to certain limits. The larger coves may be made with a special adapter that takes two molding knives as shown in the sketch. These molding knives must be ground to the correct

shape, then set up between the collars.

The second method of cutting the cove is with a core box plane. In this case the stock must be made up in a full semicircle and then cut through the center when the cove has been worked. The arcs for the inner and outer curves are drawn on the end. As much wood as possible is removed from the center by a series of saw cuts as shown in the sketch. The core box plane is designed to cut a perfect semicircle.

The third method of cutting a cove is on the circular saw. While this entails a considerable amount of setting up it is a simple method of doing the work. As with the preceding method the arcs

SAW BLADE RAISED TO THE EQUIVALENT TO THE DEPTH OF INSIDE ARC

DIA. of INSIDE ARC

PARALLEL RULE SET FOR INSIDE DIA. OF ARC, THEN PLACED ON SAW TABLE TO OBTAIN CORRECT ANGLE

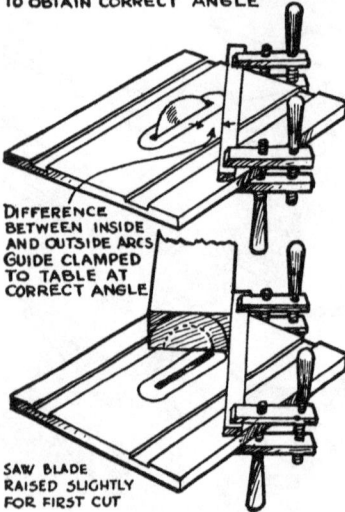

DIFFERENCE BETWEEN INSIDE AND OUTSIDE ARCS GUIDE CLAMPED TO TABLE AT CORRECT ANGLE

SAW BLADE RAISED SLIGHTLY FOR FIRST CUT

clamped to the top, at this angle, placing it the thickness of the wall of the curved piece, away from the saw blade. The saw blade is low for the first cut, and raised slightly for each succeeding cut.

The outer curve is shaped by hand. First, the corners are cut off at an angle of 45 degrees on circular saw or jointer; then finishing the work is done with a smooth plane. When completely shaped, the piece is cut down the center to produce the quarter-round corner.

Fastening this type of corner to other members may be done with dowel, mortise and tenon, tongue and groove or spline joints, as shown in the sketches.

should be laid out on the work. The saw blade is then raised to the height which is equivalent to the radius of the inside arc.

The next thing that must be determined is the angle at which the wood must enter the saw to produce the required curve. This is done by making a parallel rule of scrap stock. The distance between the inside edges of the parallel rule must be the same as the diameter of the arc that is to be cut. The parallel rule is placed over the saw blade so the teeth of the blade touch the edges of the rule. This is the angle at which the wood must enter the saw. A line is drawn along the saw table and the parallel rule is removed. A fence made of a piece of $\frac{3}{4}''$ x $1\frac{3}{4}''$ stock is

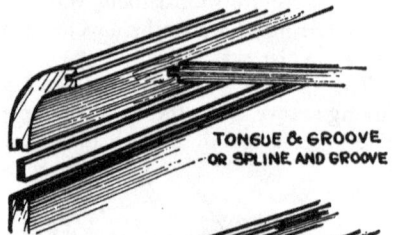

TONGUE & GROOVE OR SPLINE AND GROOVE

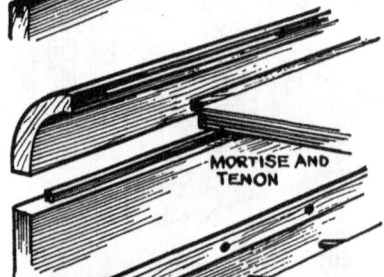

MORTISE AND TENON

DOWEL JOINT

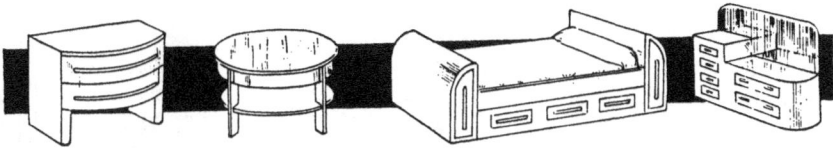

How to Make Curved Panels for Modern Furniture

THE design of many pieces of modern furniture calls for the construction of rounded corners and rounded or shaped panels. The method of making such corners was described on pages 49 and 50. The building up of rounded or shaped panels will be described here.

The theory followed in the making of a rounded or shaped panel is based on the fact that a thin piece of wood may be bent in almost any shape without the necessity of a great deal of pressure. If such a piece of wood is wet first and

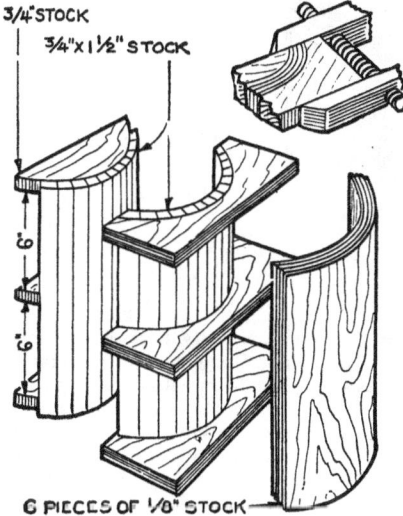

3/4"STOCK

3/4"x 1 1/2" STOCK

6 PIECES OF 1/8" STOCK

then bent and allowed to remain in that position until it is dry, it will hold that shape almost indefinitely. It can be easily understood that furniture cannot be constructed of stock so thin that it may be bent easily, but if a number of these thin pieces of stock are bent in the same shape and then glued together, the result will be a panel or a rail that will

have sufficient thickness and strength to be used for furniture.

The sketches included here illustrate three different types of forms that may be made to produce almost any shape panel or rail. While the forms in each case are only used as such, the results obtained in making the panels or rails will depend on how carefully and well constructed these forms are.

In the building up of a long panel, the arc or sweep desired should first be laid out. This arc will form one side of the form. The other side of the form should be parallel to the first arc and placed the distance apart equivalent to the thickness of the desired panel. With both these curves completed, the construction of the form itself is a simple matter. The cleats, or backing blocks as shown in the sketch, are cut to shape.

The vertical staves are cut from $\frac{3}{4}''$ stock, $1\frac{1}{2}''$ wide. The length of these staves will depend on the length of the panel being made. The staves are fastened to the cleats with $1\frac{1}{2}''$ brads and then set deeply. The convex form has the stave planed on the face so as

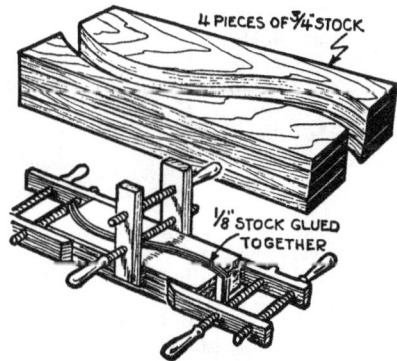

4 PIECES OF 3/4" STOCK

1/8" STOCK GLUED TOGETHER

to form a smooth round surface. When completed, the various pieces of $\frac{1}{8}''$ stock that are to be glued together should be thoroughly soaked in water, then put in the form one at a time and the form clamped together.

After each piece has been bent to shape, the faces are covered with glue, either casein or any type of cold glue,

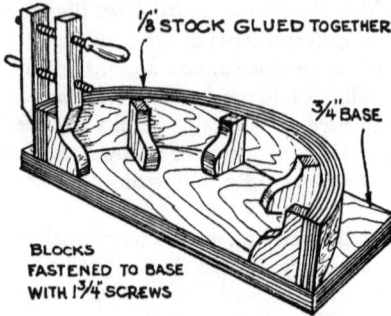

⅛" STOCK GLUED TOGETHER

¾" BASE

BLOCKS FASTENED TO BASE WITH 1¾" SCREWS

and the pieces put together back in the form. The clamps are applied again and allowed to remain on the form while the glue is setting. When the stock is removed from the form, the result will be a panel that will hold its shape.

The construction of the other two types of forms may easily be followed from the sketches. The procedure in shaping and gluing up the stock in each of these cases is the same as with the panels.

Make Wood Panels at Low Cost

FURNITURE that is both light in weight and free from warp can be constructed with the use of materials that are relatively cheap. By using the lower-priced plywood of ⅛", 3/16" or ¼" thicknesses and gluing pieces to both sides of frames made of ½" x 1½" stock as shown in Fig. 1, substantial panels ¾" to 1" thickness can be produced.

Panels made up in this manner can be sed for table tops, cabinet sides, tops, bot-

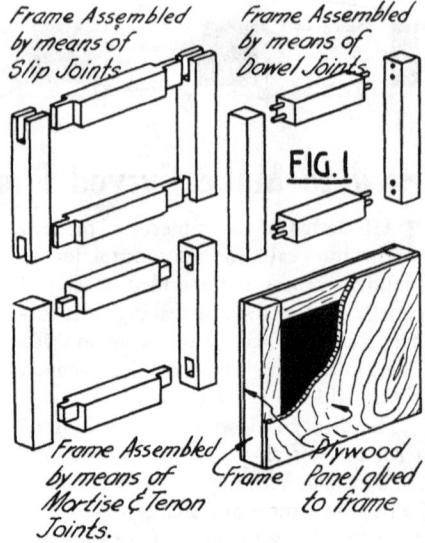

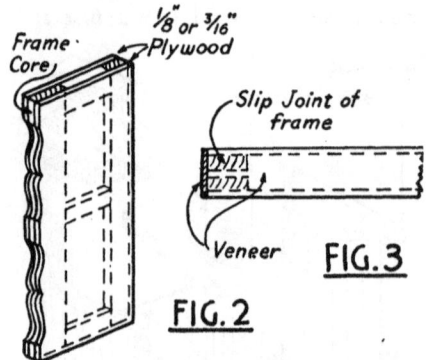

Frame Assembled by means of Slip Joints

Frame Assembled by means of Dowel Joints

FIG.1

Frame Assembled by means of Mortise & Tenon Joints.

Frame

Plywood Panel glued to frame

Frame Core

⅛" or 3/16" Plywood

Slip Joint of frame

Veneer

FIG.3

FIG.2

toms, shelves and doors, bookcase members, and, to a limited extent, members that require curved contours cut on the band saw or jig saw Panels that are to be shaped on the band saw or jig saw, however, may require frame members wider than 1½". This width will have to be determined by the contour that is to be cut as shown in Fig. 2.

Where strength is needed, as when setting shelves into a dado or gain cut in the panel, an additional rail should be added to the frame before the plywood panels are glued to it. Such rails may be set into the stiles or end rails by mortise-and-tenon or dowel joints.

The best method of constructing the frames if the panel, when completed, is to have mortises, dadoes or rabbets cut in it or the edges are to be molded, is with mortise-

and-tenon joints. Slip joints may be used if the edges are to be finished with veneer as in the case of a table top. The veneer will cover the exposed ends of the joint as shown in Fig. 3. Dowel joints may be used for assembling the frame of any panel that is not to have mortise gains or dadoes cut near the joints.

The lengths of the various frame members will depend on the size of the finished panel. These members should be cut to such a length as to produce a panel at least ½″ wider and ½″ longer than that which is required. The plywood panels that are to be applied should be the same size as this rough frame. After the panels are glued to the frame, the frame can be cut and squared to the finished size.

When gluing up the frame, the members should be held together with bar clamps. The frame should be checked for squareness before the glue has had time to set. This can be done either with a try square or by measuring the diagonal distances between the corners. If the frame is square, the diagonal distances will be alike. Should the frame be out of square, it can be corrected by shifting the clamps. When setting aside the clamped-up frame, be sure that the frame members are resting on a true plane. It may be necessary to block up under each corner of the frame as shown in Fig. 4 in order to prevent the frame from

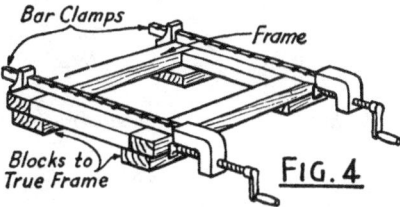

FIG. 5
Hand Screws
Frame & Panel
Pressure Strips
Veneer Press

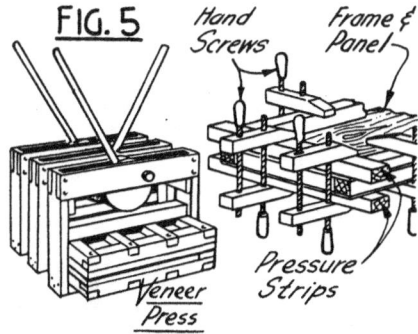

Bar Clamps
Frame
Blocks to True Frame
FIG. 4

twisting out of shape. After the clamps have been removed, plane both faces of the frame, if necessary, to remove excess glue at the joints or to bring the faces of the rails and stiles flush with one another.

Applying the panels to the frame will require the use of hand screws or a veneer press as shown in Fig. 5. The glue is spread over one face of the frame members and on all sections of one plywood piece that is to come in contact with the frame members. The panel is placed over the frame, which is then turned over, and the opposite face of the frame and the panel which is to be applied to it are treated in the same manner. The frame, with its panels in place, is clamped or placed in a

veneer press and pressure is applied.

The system outlined here is an inexpensive means of producing what appears to be a thick panel. The thin plywood selected for covering the frame can be faced one side with mahogany, walnut or any other fine cabinet wood. This grade of plywood costs a good deal less than solid wood or heavier plywood panels.

Simplified Plywood Furniture

IT IS so easy to construct furniture from plywood that many persons are doing so where they have no workshop facilities and only a few hand tools. This is especially true in the case of apartment dwellers, but there are also many young couples who have moved into new houses and wish to furnish them quickly, yet have not yet set up a workshop or acquired any power tools.

Now, while the use of plywood simplifies construction greatly, there are still two problems which trouble the beginner. One is how to conceal the raw edges of the material, particularly if the furniture is to have a natural rather than a painted or enameled finish. The other is how to make legs or corner posts and attach the plywood to them in some convenient and reasonably presentable way.

Both these problems may be readily solved, provided one does not insist on a perfectly flat, unbroken, veneered treatment such as is found in modern-style television cabinets and similar factory-made furniture.

All that it is necessary to do, in addition to obtaining the plywood panels and any solid lumber for shelves and other parts, is to get from a lumberyard a supply of so-called corner molding and some square stock. The molding is shaped as shown in Fig. 1. A common size is 1¼″ x 1¼″

with a wood thickness of about ¼" The square stock should be purchased of a size to fit inside the molding. For a molding of the size mentioned, ¾" square stock is usually the most suitable, but 1" square will do as it can easily be planed as required, or strips can be ripped from a ¾" thick board and planed by hand. So few strips are required that this is a minor matter.

Suppose, for example, that you are making a cabinet which requires legs and several shelves. The cabinet proper can be made like a box from ¼" or thicker plywood, depending upon its size. The parts must be measured accurately and cut perfectly square. They can be glued and well nailed with small brads, plenty of which may be used since they will not show. There will be a large panel for the back, two panels for the sides and one or more narrow members to go across the front, depending upon the design that is being followed.

It is most important, of course, to make sure that the assembly is square. In the absence of a steel square or large try-square, the checking can be done by measuring diagonally from corner to corner. If both diagonals are the same, the cabinet is square.

Four pieces of the corner molding are now cut the full height of the cabinet (less the thickness of the top, which is applied last, from the floor. These are glued in place as shown in Fig. 2. If the gluing is properly done with a first-class glue, brads are hardly necessary, but a few may be used or some thin, small screws driven from inside through the plywood into the corner molding.

The next step is to cut four filler blocks from the square stock for the bottom of the legs. These should be of the correct length to support the bottom of the cabinet or the lowest shelf. They are glued and lightly bradded into the legs as shown in Fig. 3. If the lower part of the legs will show, the blocks should fill out the molding to a perfect square and may either be planed down or built out with filler pieces as necessary to accomplish this.

The cabinet bottom or lowest shelf is then cut to fit inside the cabinet and placed on the filler blocks. Another set of blocks is next prepared to fill in behind the legs up to the second shelf. The second shelf is fitted and inserted in the same way, and this method of construction is continued until the cabinet has been completed, as indicated in Fig. 4. It will then be a

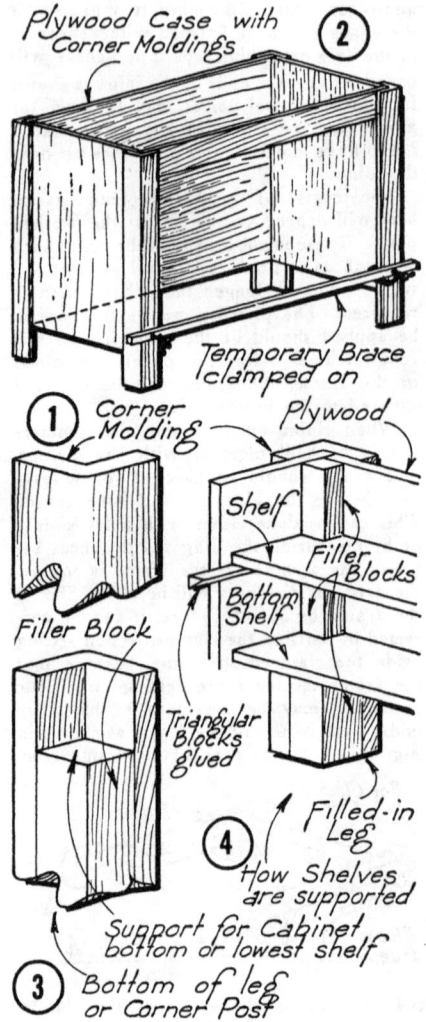

Plywood Case with Corner Moldings ②

Temporary Brace clamped on

① Corner Molding — Plywood

Shelf

Filler Block

Filler Blocks

Bottom Shelf

Triangular Blocks glued

Filled-in Leg

④ How Shelves are supported

Support for Cabinet bottom or lowest shelf

③ Bottom of leg or Corner Post

strong unit with what amounts to four substantial square legs with shelves locked in as if with mortise-and-tenoned or other well-made joints.

If there are places where the shelves need additional support, small triangular gluing blocks may be glued against the underside of the shelves and the side and back panels as shown in Fig. 4. Lengths of the square stock may also be glued in where necessary to strengthen the assembly, to provide drawer runners and for other purposes.

When the top is finally placed on the cabinet, the method of construction will be well concealed and, provided the design of the piece of furniture is attractive, no one will suspect that it has been built by such a simple and unorthodox method without the use of carefully fitted joints.

Making Cedar Panels

WHEN the craftsman wants cedar paneling for a particular shop project, he is faced with the fact that most cedar stock comes in the form of closet lining which is $5/16''$ thick and $2\frac{1}{4}''$ wide, with edges tongued and grooved.

To convert cedar lining into panels of whatever width is desired, it will be neces-

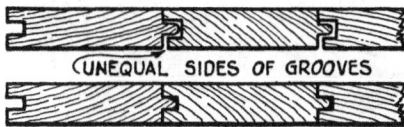

UNEQUAL SIDES OF GROOVES

sary to joint the grooved edge, because most of this stock has unequal projecting edges. After the edge has been jointed to bring these projections in line, the pieces are glued and clamped in the usual manner. Afterwards the complete panel is sanded on both faces.

Pointers on Using Moldings

AMATEUR woodworkers are using moldings more extensively now that so many of them have either a woodworking shaper, a molding head for use with the bench saw, or a special shaping spindle and cutters for the drill press. This enables them to embellish their woodwork in many ways, but there is one important thing to keep in mind: a molding is good only when it is used appropriately.

You can't judge a molding merely by its beautiful profile when laid out full size on a sheet of drawing paper. It is important to consider where the molding is to be used and from what angle it will be viewed.

Some moldings are seen only from below, as those at the top of a tall bookcase or

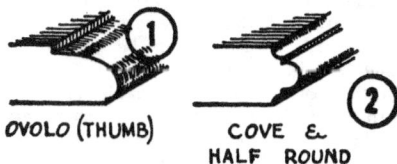

OVOLO (THUMB)   COVE &
                 HALF ROUND

cabinet, whereas base moldings are seen only from above. Others, as the molding around the top of a table, are seen mainly, but not entirely, from above. Still others, such as moldings around a large door panel, are seen from all angles. This seems very elementary and obvious, yet it is often overlooked with the result that moldings which are attractive in themselves do not appear to advantage on the furniture or other woodwork on which they are used.

The so-called thumb molding shown in Fig. 1, for example, would be appropriate

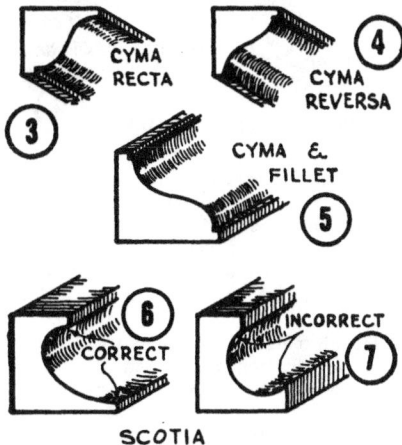

SCOTIA

for use around a table top. That shown in Fig. 2 would also be suitable, but should not be placed above the eye level around the top of a tall cabinet. On the other hand, the cyma recta or ogee in Fig. 3 is a good molding for use in a cornice. A similar molding may be used with the fillet, or square member, at the top and with the curves reversed, when it is known as a cyma reversa (Fig. 4). Turned the other way round, this type of molding serves to ornament a base member as in Fig. 5.

Another point to observe in the design of moldings is that the curves should meet the horizontal and vertical parts, or the fillets, as they are usually called, at a right angle, or approximately so. Figure 6, for example, is good, whereas Fig. 7 is bad. In other words, the profile should be clean-cut and the various elements should be definitely separated so that clear shadows will be thrown; in fact, the shadows are what give a molding character.

Another precaution to take is to see that the elements are not monotonously alike or all of the same relative size. This is particularly important to keep in mind when several standard cutters are being used to shape a compound molding. Note how much superior Fig. 8 is to Fig. 9.

Some woodworking moldings are based on the circle, as the conventional quarter-round and half-round, but the more complicated moldings look better if the curves are of the more subtle or freehand type

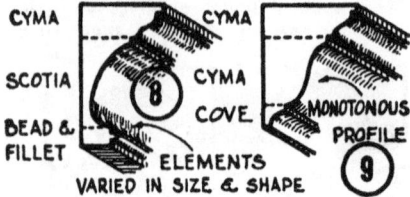

CYMA
CYMA
SCOTIA
CYMA
BEAD &
COVE
FILLET
ELEMENTS
VARIED IN SIZE & SHAPE
MONOTONOUS
PROFILE
8
9

that cannot be drawn with a compass. Molding cutters, however, are designed with this in mind and are now provided in such a variety of shapes that the home craftsman can obtain beautiful profiles in almost unlimited combinations by using them.

Although moldings are intended as ornaments, they are sometimes used for purely utilitarian purposes, especially in modern cabinets, chests of drawers and desks. This is when they are cut into the edges of doors and drawers to give a convenient finger grip or handhold. Here their shape, usually a simple cove, is dictated purely by their function.

Constructing Utility Tables

WORKTABLES or utility tables of reasonable size can be built quickly and simply from ordinary boards by using the leg construction illustrated. For use in the workshop, on porches and in playrooms, game rooms, summer cottages, auto camps and the like, tables made in this way are quite adequate and are not unsightly if neatly painted or stained and varnished. They have the additional advantage that they can be taken apart expeditiously for shipment or storage.

Each leg consists of two tapered pieces cut from a ¾" board—or even thinner stock in the case of children's play tables and other very small tables. The parts are glued and nailed together with finishing brads along their straight edges.

The four rails and the lower stretchers at

each end are fastened inside the legs with flathead screws as shown in the detail drawing. If there is no intention of ever taking the table apart, glue should also be used for additional strength.

Large tables or those which are to be subjected to hard usage may be braced with a lower shelf of any desired width. This is screwed on top of the stretchers.

The boards which form the top are fastened to three or more cleats as indicated. If the end cleats are spaced to fit snugly between the end rails, the table top

LEG
WORKTABLE MADE ENTIRELY OF ¾" BOARDS
RAILS FASTENED TO LEGS WITH SCREWS
3 OR MORE BATTENS FASTENED UNDER TOP WITH ROUNDHEAD SCREW

is simply dropped into place. It can then be removed quickly when the table is to be taken apart. If preferred, the top may be fastened permanently with a few screws driven from the inside through the end cleats into the end rails.

Give the table a paint or varnish finish and apply linoleum to the top, if desired.

How to Plane Wood Very Thin

FOR model making, strips of very thin wood are often required. Standard veneers, which are 1/28" thick are readily obtainable in maple, walnut, mahogany, teak, ebony and other suitable woods from craftwork supply houses, and boxwood—a favorite with model makers—is usually available in 1/24" and 1/16" thicknesses. However, still thinner pieces are sometimes needed. These can be planed by hand if a little care is taken.

Either saw a piece of maple or other hard wood about ⅛" thick, or select a very flat, perfect piece of veneer and fasten it to a smooth, flat board or scrap of

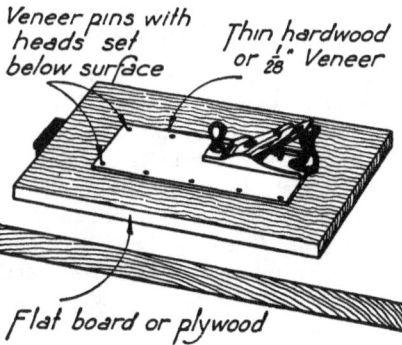

Veneer pins with heads set below surface — Thin hardwood or 1/28" Veneer

Flat board or plywood

thick plywood with a few veneer pins or small, thin brads. If the wood has a tendency to split, drill holes or stick small patches of veneer tape or Scotch tape on the surface before driving the nails. Set the heads slightly below the surface. Now take a shaving or two off the surface with a very sharp, fine-set plane. Drive the heads of the nails slightly deeper and remove a few more shavings, continuing this way until the wood is as thin as desired. By this method a piece of 1/28" close-grained hardwood veneer such as maple can be reduced to about half that thickness without breaking or splitting the wood.

Rockers Made by Laminating

WHEN repairing or constructing a rocking chair, the craftsman usually finds that constructing the rockers offers quite a problem if suitable material is not available. One method that will be found

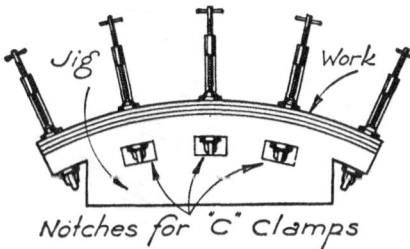

Jig — Work

Notches for "C" Clamps

highly satisfactory is to make the rockers by laminating several pieces of thin stock.

The first step is to make a form to hold the strips at the desired curvature until the glue sets. Using the old rocker as a template, mark the desired curvature on the face of 2 x 8 stock and saw or remove the waste wood down to line. It is best

to give just a little more curvature than old rocker to allow for slight spring back.

Next, rip out several strips for each rocker $\frac{3}{16}$" x $1\frac{3}{4}$" x 40" long. Apply glue on both sides of one strip, then place the other two strips on each side of glued surface. The strips are held on the jig form by means of C-clamps. Notches are cut in the jig to accommodate the clamps.

White poplar or oak are good material to use for the strips. Of course, the size of strips may vary somewhat from those given to suit the needs of the craftsman. However, it is better to use four strips to get the desired thickness, if more than three are needed, rather than increase the thickness of each strip.

Sanding Small Flat Surfaces

WHEN very small pieces of wood have to be sanded by hand, it is usually better to lay a sheet of sandpaper on the workbench and rub the work on it. This is

not only more convenient, but it insures flatter surfaces.

The same principle may be used in filing small, flat surfaces. It takes considerable skill to avoid rounding such surfaces if the work is held in the vise in the usual way, but the other method where the file lies flat on the bench is comparatively easy. For this work, choose a flat, smooth-cut file; and if a parallel or equaling file, which has no taper, is available, use it.

Splicing Short Fence Rails

WHEN erecting a picket or lawn-wire fence, it will often prove advantageous to splice the rails as shown in the sketch. In this way, 2 x 4's of odd lengths that do not

match the spaces between the posts can be used without unsightly reinforcing battens. Wasteful cutting of rails to fit between posts is also eliminated.

Make the splices 8" to 10" long, and use 4" or 4½" carriage bolts, spaced not less than 2" from the ends. If either rail shows

57

$\frac{3}{16}'' \times 4''$ CARRIAGE BOLTS

8"

RAILS MADE OF
2"x 4" STOCK

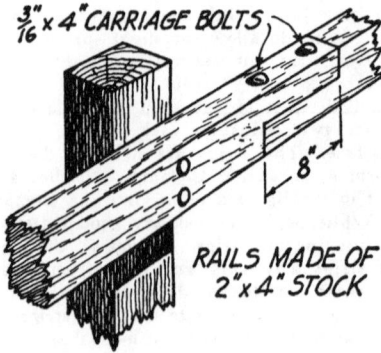

a tendency to split up from the splice, use another bolt 2" above the cut. It is a good idea to place a larger washer under the nut of each bolt to avoid the crushing action of the bolt on the wood as it is tightened.

Box Feet Cut from Molding

NEAT-LOOKING wooden feet for cigarette boxes, trinket boxes and other small boxes, as well as for the baseboards of instruments, pipe racks and the like, can be made from a scrap of almost any available stock molding as shown. Cut V-shaped pieces from the molding in a miter box and glue them under the corners. If the box or baseboard is already finished, the feet should be finished to match before being applied.

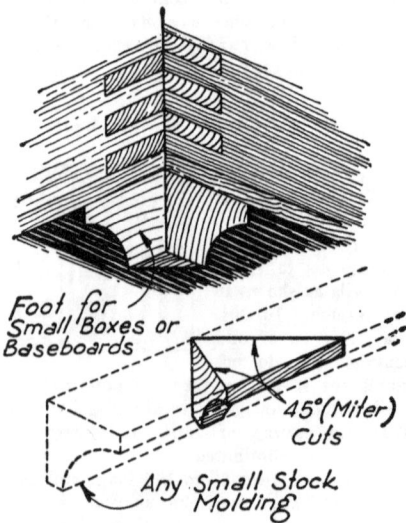

Foot for
Small Boxes or
Baseboards

45°(Miter)
Cuts

Any Small Stock
Molding

Seamless Tubing Used for Modern Furniture Is Bent Over Wood Forms

MUCH modern furniture is built of bent seamless tubing. For the craftsman who would like to undertake the construction of a piece designed to use such material, the first thing that is required is a form, over which the tubing is bent. There is always a certain amount of spring in a piece of metal that is being bent; therefore when making the bend, the form over which it is worked, should be sharper than the desired curve.

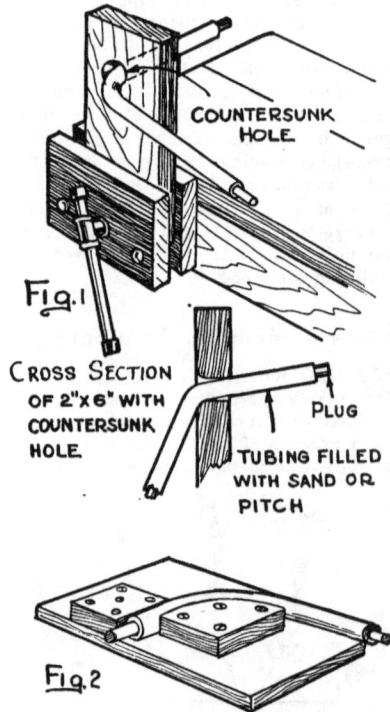

COUNTERSUNK
HOLE.

Fig. 1

CROSS SECTION
OF 2"x 6" WITH
COUNTERSUNK
HOLE.

PLUG

TUBING FILLED
WITH SAND OR
PITCH

Fig. 2

There are two types of forms shown in the drawing. One is a simple form made of a piece of 2" x 6" with a countersunk hole in it a little larger than the tubing that is to be bent. See Fig. 1. This may be used for sharp bends that are more than 90 degrees. The second form is made of three pieces of stock, two of which are mounted to the third piece with screws. See Fig. 2. This form can be used for making any type of bend, at any angle desired, depending on the shape of the block.

The problem of keeping out the kinks may now be considered. One of the simplest methods of doing this is to pack the inside of the tube with hot sand. A plug will have to be inserted in one end while the sand is poured in from the other. It may be packed by beating the sides of the tube with a soft wood block. When the tube has been filled another plug is inserted in the other end. When this has been done, it will be found that the tube will bend without flattening or kinking.

Simplest Way to Bend Wood Panels

CURVED panels are often required in construction of pieces designed along modern lines. Commercially these panels are usually steamed and bent in forming presses, but for the home craftsman this method of producing a curved panel is out of the question. The same effect can be ob-

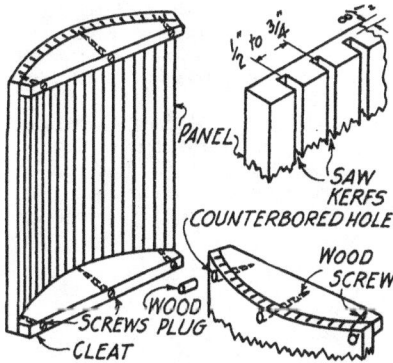

PANEL

SAW KERFS

COUNTERBORED HOLE

WOOD SCREW

WOOD PLUG

SCREWS

CLEAT

tained in the home workshop when a bench saw is used to make a series of saw kerfs ½" to ¾" apart and to a depth of ⅛" in the unexposed face of the stock. The curve that the panel is required to take is the controlling factor in the spacing of the saw kerfs. The sharper the bend, the closer must be the saw kerfs. Wood removed by the saw makes room for compression of the panel.

By the use of this method it is possible to shape plywood or solid stock of ¾" thickness to an arc having a radius as small as 12". Naturally, this system can be used only when one face of the panel can be concealed.

A panel prepared in such a manner should be fastened to cleats cut to the shape of the curve. The screws used to fasten the panel to the cleats may be driven through the cleat and into the back of the panel or may be driven through the panel and into the cleat. If the latter method is used, it is advisable to counterbore the screw hole and then, after the screw has been driven, set a wood plug in the counterbore to cover the head of the screw.

Saw-Kerf Method of Bending

IN CONSTRUCTING certain types of built-in furniture, home bars and the like, and also when making repairs to round porch columns, rounded stairs and similar work, it is sometimes necessary to bend boards or molding to a predetermined radius.

When the cuts are made by guesswork, however, they are not likely to be spaced properly. If they are irregular, or if some are made deeper than others, the wood will bend unevenly and the finished work may reveal unsightly ribs or flat surfaces. For greatest strength and permanence, it is also important that the cuts be spaced so that they will close up along their inner edges when the part is bent. Then, if thick casein glue is used liberally in the saw kerfs before fastening the part in place, the whole will become a strong, rigid unit.

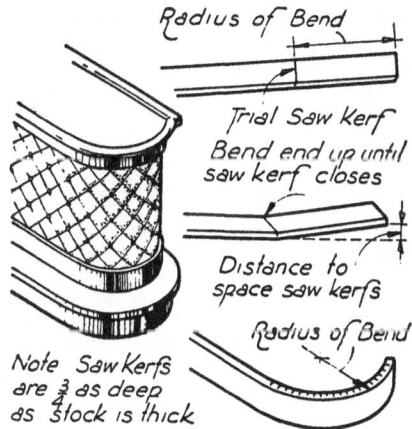

Radius of Bend

Trial Saw Kerf
Bend end up until saw kerf closes

Distance to space saw kerfs

Radius of Bend

Note Saw Kerfs are ¾ as deep as stock is thick

The great difficulty in this work is to figure out how deep and far apart to make the saw kerfs. Here is a good way to do this:

Measure the radius to which the work is to be bent and lay out this distance from one end of the board or molding, as illustrated. At this point make a saw cut part way through the stock. The depth is usually about three fourths the thickness of the wood, but for relatively sharp bends it may have to be slightly more.

Now lay the board or molding flat on the floor or workbench and lift up the end until the edges of the saw cut come together, as shown somewhat exaggerated in the drawing. Note the exact distance you have raised the end. Whatever this distance is, it represents the ideal spacing between the saw kerfs. Make the cuts this distance apart along the entire distance where the work is to be bent. Use the same saw and take care, of course, to have the kerfs all the same depth as the first trial cut.

Drawer Locks Are Easy to Fit

AMATEUR cabinetmakers frequently omit drawer locks in the desks, cabinets, dressers, lowboys and other pieces of furniture they make. Sometimes, however, it is desirable to provide at least one drawer in a piece of furniture with a good lock.

To fit a drawer lock of any of the ordinary varieties, such as the one shown in Fig. 1, is comparatively easy. There is only one dimension which has to be

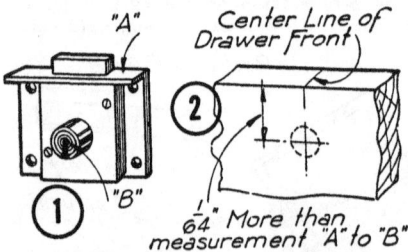

measured and accurately observed, and that is the distance from the top or selvedge A of the lock to the center of the tube or cylinder B (or to the pin in the center of the keyhole if the lock is of the style which has no cylinder). This distance is then marked on the center line of the drawer front, measuring down from the upper edge as in Fig. 2. An experienced

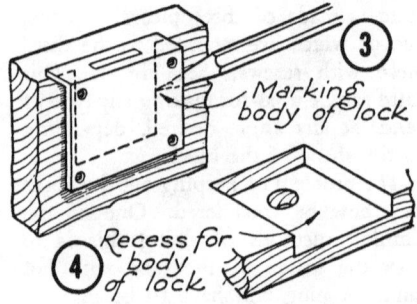

cabinetmaker will add about $\frac{1}{64}$" or a trifle more to the measurement so that the lock selvedge will be sunk that much below the top edge of the drawer front. This is in case the drawer may have to have a shaving removed from that edge after the lock is fitted. It is a precautionary allowance.

At the point marked, a hole is bored a snug fit for the lock's cylinder. If the lock is of the simpler variety which has no cylinder, a $\frac{1}{4}$" or smaller hole is bored; it merely provides passage for the round part of the key and forms the upper portion of the keyhole.

Now put the cylinder or the keyhole pin of the lock centrally into the hole from the back. Mark around the front or smaller plate of the lock as shown in Fig. 3. Cut or rout out a recess deep enough to receive the body of the lock as in Fig. 4.

After placing the lock in this recess, mark around the selvedge or edge plate as in Fig. 5. Use a very hard, sharp pencil or a knife. Cut the recess for the selvedge as in Fig. 6.

If desired, another shallow recess may be cut in the back of the drawer front so that the back plate of the lock can be set in flush, but this is rarely done.

Nothing remains except to fasten the

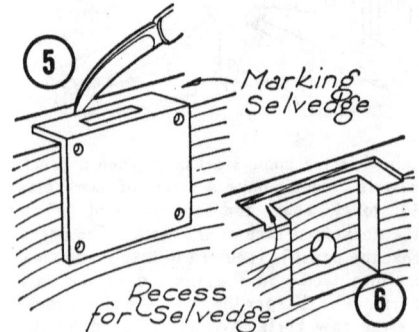

lock in place if it is of the type shown in Fig. 1. If, however, the lock is of the common keyhole variety, a keyhole must be cut out in the wood large enough for the key or for a rim escutcheon such as shown at A in Fig. 7. Such an escutcheon

Escutcheons

requires careful fitting and is not often used except in very fine work. Ordinarily the keyhole is finished with a plate escutcheon such as those shown at B, Fig. 7.

To receive the bolt, a hole will have to be chiseled in the upper drawer rail, desk top or whatever wooden part is immediately above the drawer. To mark the location, use the key to turn the bolt out and rub a soft black pencil or crayon over the face of the bolt, or brush on some paint. Now turn the bolt down, close the drawer and turn the bolt up hard against the wood. This will mark the position and size of the mortise.

Locating Locks on Doors

MOST manufacturers of modern-type door locks provide a template, with the lock set, which is used for locating the various holes that must be bored. In order to use such a template and at the same time position the holes for the lock set accurately, cut away the template at the fold as shown in the photograph. Through the use of this opening, no difficulty will be encountered in lining up the center line on the template with the one previously established on the door.

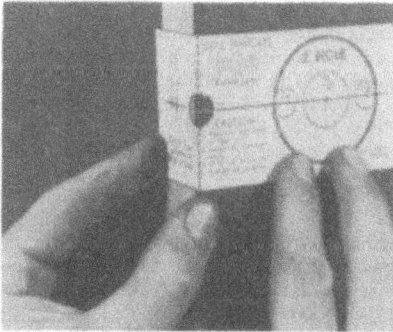

Hinging Console-Table Tops

WHEN using so-called "invisible" hinges to hinge the two halves of a console-table top and for other similar purposes, be sure to place a sheet of cardboard between the two parts of the top at the time one is laid over the other while you are locating the hinges and marking the hole centers. The use of the cardboard will insure sufficient clearance so there will be no danger that the hinged joint will bind.

Hole Markers for Fitting Hinges Made from Wood Screws

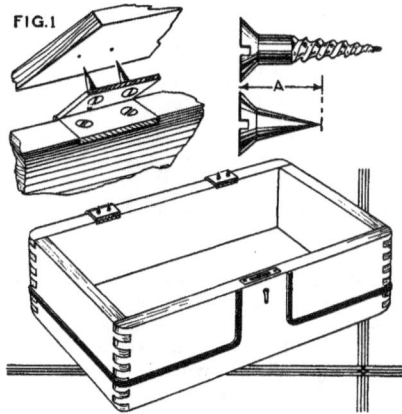

FIG.1

ANY piece of cabinet work which is to be equipped with a hinged door or lid must be hinged accurately or the value of the entire piece is destroyed. Simple hole markers made from wood screws will eliminate the danger. One pair of markers made from small wood screws will serve for several common sizes of hinges.

Hold a screw with a pair of pliers while grinding the point of the screw to resemble Fig. A in the drawing. Two are required. Locate, drill holes and attach one leaf of the hinge to the cabinet. Then insert the markers in the second leaf and with a piece of cardboard slipped between the leaves to make them parallel, lay the lid in the correct position. Where the markers locate points, as in Fig. 1, drill holes for screws. Then recess the lid for the leaf.

Repairing Worn Hinge Seats

THE wood around the hinge seats of very old doors, or doors that have been subjected to excessive abuse, become so worn and split that it is necessary to patch

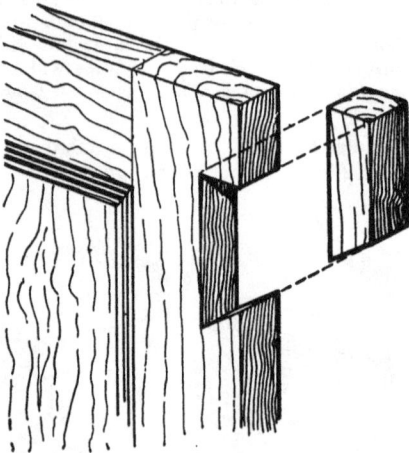

the hinge edge of the door. These patches are often cut in straight, but it is much better to glue in dovetail patches as shown. When the glue is hard, new hinge seats can be cut and there will be no danger that the patches will ever work loose.

Battered Furniture Corners

OLD tables, chests of drawers and other antique pieces of furniture are sometimes unsightly because one or more corners of the top have become badly battered by reason of rough handling in moving or other accidents. A corner injury of this type may look something like Fig. 1. It is, of course, impossible to make a satisfactory repair of such severe damage with either composition wood or stick shellac.

The best method is to cut the corner off on the diagonal, following the direction of the grain. The closer the cut parallels the grain, the less conspicuous the patch will be. Indeed, this is a basic rule in patching old furniture; avoid cuts directly across the grain as far as possible because they are the ones which will show up badly no matter how carefully the refinishing is done.

The cut edge should be planed straight and smooth. The next step is to select a scrap of wood of the same kind as the

original top and glue it in place as shown in Fig. 2. A high-quality, durable, moisture-resistant glue should be used and the piece clamped securely by any convenient method. Leave the joint at least overnight to allow the glue to harden.

After the patch has been planed to the approximate shape, the molded edge, if it is molded, can be duplicated on the patch with chisels, gouges and sandpaper as shown in Fig. 3. In all such work, avoid

damaging the original finish on the old wood unless the finish is to be stripped off and the whole top refinished completely.

To color and finish a patch of this type to match the old finish is perhaps the most difficult part of the work, unless modern materials and methods are used. If walnut, mahogany or other open-grained wood has been used, it is necessary to apply first a paste wood filler of a color somewhat lighter than the original finish. Natural paste filler can be colored for this purpose with oil colors of the type sold in tubes or with dry pigments. When the filler is thoroughly dry, a wash coat of very thin shellac is brushed on the patch. This is sanded lightly when dry.

Next, the whole top is given a light coat of refinisher's padding lacquer applied in circles or figure 8's with a pad. The same padding lacquer is then used with pigmented stain powders to bring the patch to an exact match in color with the remainder of the surface. A little careful blending will conceal the joint almost perfectly.

After another light sanding, the entire surface is repadded with the lacquer to whatever degree of gloss is desired. If necessary, the work can be rubbed down with fine pumice stone and oil to a satin finish or with rottenstone and oil to give a high polish, but as a rule the padding lacquer alone will be satisfactory. Expert refinishers often dilute the padding lacquer with an equal quantity of solvent for the final padding when a high-gloss finish is required.

How to Repair Cracked Panels

IN RESTORING old furniture such as chests of drawers, cabinets of various types and wardrobes, it is frequently necessary to repair unsightly cracks in the wide end members or panels. Before the day of plywood, these parts were made from solid stock, which was very likely to crack in the course of time unless the construction was so skillfully designed that the pieces were free to shrink and expand at will.

The question is: How can the cracks be repaired without taking the piece of furniture apart?

If the cracked member is the wide end of a chest of drawers, as shown in Fig. 1, and the cracks are too large to be patched with stick shellac, the best procedure is to widen the splits carefully to their very end with a small saw. Select a piece of matching wood about the same width as the thickness of the part being repaired, and cut a strip slightly thicker than the widest part of the crack. Bevel this strip with a plane so that it can be inserted without difficulty into the crack, yet will close

the crack completely when hammered into place. Apply glue to the edges of the crack with a sliver of wood or a thin knife blade; also brush glue on both sides of the slim wedge. When this piece has been driven in and the glue has set hard, the surplus wood can be trimmed off with a chisel and the patch sanded flush with the surface.

When a door panel or other panel in a frame has cracked, it may be possible in some cases to remove it by taking out the molding or strips which hold one side in place. In that case, glue can be inserted in the cracks and the panel clamped tightly enough to close them. If they are too wide for this, thin wedge strips can be fitted as previously suggested. When repaired, the panel can be fastened back in place.

The panel in many instances, however, is set in grooves and cannot be removed. If it is in a door or placed where the back is accessible—and if the splits are narrow ones—simply screw small blocks near the edges as shown in Fig. 2 and use wedges

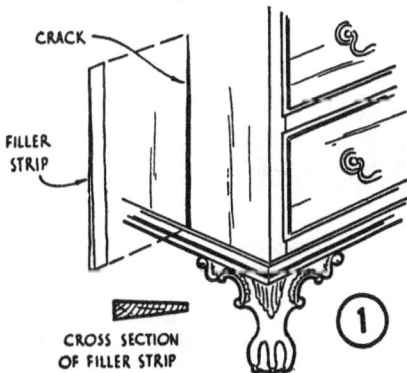

INSIDE OF DOOR OR PANEL FRAME

to apply the necessary pressure to force the cracks shut. Be sure, of course, that the frame joints are firmly fastened or the pressure may cause them to open. If the cracks are so wide that it is difficult to draw them together and there is danger that they would reopen in time in spite of the glue, they should be filled with wood strips.

When cracks have been repaired with new wood, a favorite professional method of refinishing the work is as follows: Clean the entire surface to remove dirt, wax and furniture polish. Then restore its luster by applying a light coat of padding lacquer over all. Next mix stain powders with a little of the same lacquer to match the old finish as perfectly as possible. Apply this to the new wood with a small, fine-pointed camel's-hair brush. When this is dry, which takes only a short time, sand the patches lightly with No. 7/0 garnet paper and finish the entire surface with a final coat of the padding lacquer.

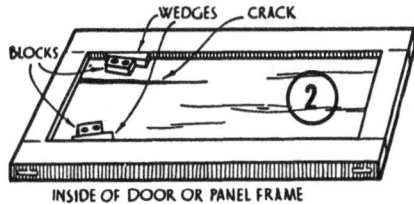

CRACK

FILLER STRIP

CROSS SECTION OF FILLER STRIP

Loosened Chair Legs Tightened with Long Screw Driven thru Corner Block

CHAIRS sometimes become wabbly through reckless use or extremely long service. Usually they are left in disrepair until the joints become worn. The remedy in this case is to be found

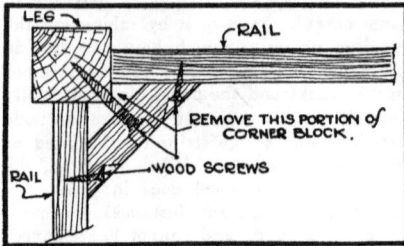

LEG — RAIL

REMOVE THIS PORTION of CORNER BLOCK.

RAIL — WOOD SCREWS

in the customary corner brace under the seat. Generally these blocks are originally cut to fill the entire corner. Screws are driven through the blocks and into the rails to secure them in place.

With a little change in these blocks they may be made to hold the leg in place far better than before. Take the block out by removing the two screws that hold it in place, then cut the corner off so that the block is not touching the leg, as shown in the sketch. Obtain a wood screw long enough to pass through the block of wood and into the leg. A hole is bored in the block large enough to permit the screw to pass through. The corner block is smeared with good glue and put back in place with two screws that hold it to the rails. The long screw is then driven into the leg last. In this manner the leg is pulled tightly against the end of the rails and held there more securely.

How to Bore Out Old Dowels

WHEN repairing chairs and other furniture, it is frequently necessary to bore out dowels which have either broken or been cut off in taking the piece apart. If new dowels of the same size are to be used, it is best to bore out the old dowels with a bit one size smaller—for example, a No. 5 bit for a $\frac{3}{8}$" dowel. Then use a sharp-pointed tool such as an awl to pry and chip away the thin remaining wall of the old dowel. In this way, the original hole may be used again. On the other hand, if an attempt is made to bore out the old dowel with a bit of the same size, the bit is very likely to run off center or at a slight angle and thus cause difficulty in assembling the work later.

Regluing Loose Chair Legs

REGARDLESS of how good the glue is, there has rarely been a chair built in which the legs, and stretchers too, have been assembled with glue that will not eventu-

Coat with glue and drive in

ally loosen or come apart. No matter how well or how often we repair them with glue alone, the joints are still likely to loosen in time.

If a narrow slot is cut in the top end of the leg, or the end of the stretcher, and a short, thin, wooden wedge is set in with glue as shown, and the tenon is also coated with glue as usual, the piece may be driven in tight. After that, it will be necessary to break the chair to remove the leg. Driving the leg in forces the glue-coated wedge down into the top of the leg and expands it so tightly in the socket that it just can't come out.

Tightening Loose Drawer Knobs

AFTER a period of time, drawer knobs held in place by a machine screw that passes through the drawer front and into the back of the knob often become loose and mar the finish near them. When tightening the screw from the inside fails to tighten the knob, it is an indication that the end of the machine screw is touching the bottom of the hole in the knob. To remedy this condition, remove the machine screw and cut off about $\frac{1}{4}$" of it with a hack saw. This sawed end should be filed to remove the burr before the screw is replaced in the knob.

Some wooden drawer knobs that are secured with machine screws have threads cut into the wood. Frequently these wood threads become stripped, with the result that the knob is not only loose but invariably comes off whenever the drawer is pulled open. The simplest way to refasten such a knob to the drawer front is to replace the machine screw with a regular wood screw, either flat or roundheaded, having a diameter large enough to be driven tightly into the hole in the knob. When choosing such a wood screw, obtain one of a length that will not pass through the knob.

Hints on Repairing Drawers

DRAWERS in old chests, desks and secretaries often have a narrow, slightly projecting molding around the front edges. This is called a "cocked bead." Parts of this bead are frequently broken off or badly damaged.

A repair can be made by cutting back the molding as shown at A in Fig. 1 and replacing the missing parts with strips of the same wood, planed to the same thickness, but slightly wider. These are

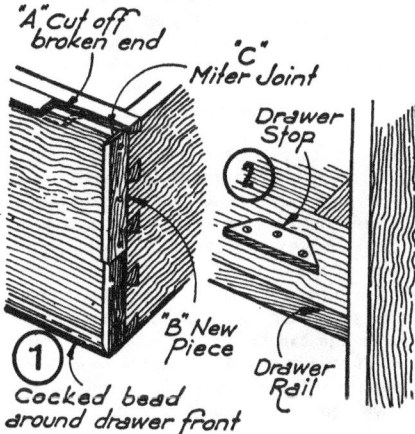

"A" cut off broken end
"C" Miter Joint
Drawer Stop
"B" New Piece
Drawer Rail
(1) Cocked bead around drawer front

fastened with glue and small brads as at B. If a corner has to be repaired, the joint should be mitered as at C. When the glue is hard, the projecting edges of the new pieces are dressed and sanded to conform to the shape of the old bead, and finished to match it in both color and surface.

The drawer stops are frequently worn or missing in old furniture. They may be

easily replaced with small blocks as in Fig. 2. These should be thick enough to stop the drawer properly, but should not rub against the drawer bottom. They must be located accurately and fastened with both glue and nails.

How to Patch Broken Carvings

ONE of the most difficult repair jobs that an amateur craftsman is likely to encounter is the replacing of a part broken off an intricate carved ornament or highly embossed molding.

The best method, if a piece is valuable and has genuine wood carving rather than imitation (embossed) carving, is to cut out the damaged portion, glue in a solid piece of matching wood and carve it by hand. This requires time and skill.

A more common and easier method is to make a mold from an undamaged part of the carving—or, in the case of a furniture leg, from one of the undamaged legs

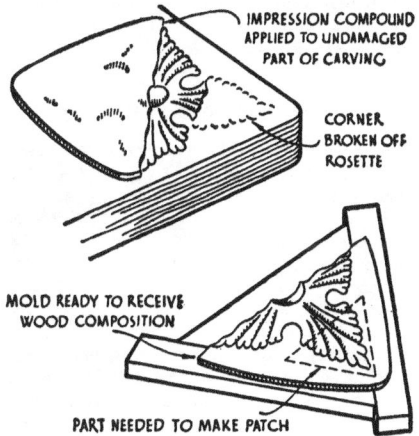

IMPRESSION COMPOUND APPLIED TO UNDAMAGED PART OF CARVING

CORNER BROKEN OFF ROSETTE

MOLD READY TO RECEIVE WOOD COMPOSITION

PART NEEDED TO MAKE PATCH

—and prepare a casting, which is then carefully fitted to the broken-away section and finished to match.

When this is attempted, the first question is what to use for making the mold. Various compounds will serve, such as a mixture of 4 oz. melted beeswax, 1 oz. olive oil and 4 oz. of starch, but the most convenient and satisfactory is probably what is known as "red dental impression compound." Your dentist usually will be glad to supply you with a small quantity. It can, of course, be used repeatedly.

After this compound has been softened

in hot water, it is flattened into a sheet at least $\frac{1}{8}''$ thick. The part of the carving selected for copying is then lightly oiled. The compound is dipped again in very hot water and immediately pressed on the carving with the aid of a cloth wrung out in hot water.

Allow the compound to harden before removing it. Then support it upside down in any convenient way. If this is difficult to do with cardboard and scraps of wood, simply turn the mold face down in a small cardboard box and pour plaster of Paris over it to form a strong, thick backing.

The mold, after being lightly oiled, can be filled with any suitable wood compound or crack filler. If the repair is being made to an ornate picture frame or other piece where strength is not required, plaster of Paris, artist's gesso or a mixture of whiting, glue size and a little varnish may be used instead of the wood compound.

Before the casting is entirely hard, remove it cautiously from the mold, reheating the impression compound with hot water if necessary. Let the casting set hard, then trim it to fit the work. Glue it in place and later fill any crevices or blemishes with crack filler and finish.

Reglue Before Refinishing

WHEN an old piece of furniture has to be refinished completely and also requires a lot of patching, regluing of joints and other work, it is a good idea to do the necessary patching and regluing before removing the old finish. Whatever surplus glue has been squeezed out will then come off when the old finish is removed and no glue stains or scraper marks will be left. If the process is reversed, the glue will have to be used much more cautiously and great pains taken to scrape off any residue in order to avoid glue marks when the new finish is applied.

Simple Way to Locate Wall Studs

QUITE often the householder is faced with the problem of hanging a heavy mirror, a large picture or a shelf. This job makes it necessary to have the hanger anchored to a stud behind the plastered wall.

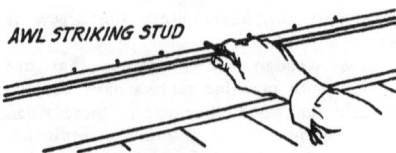

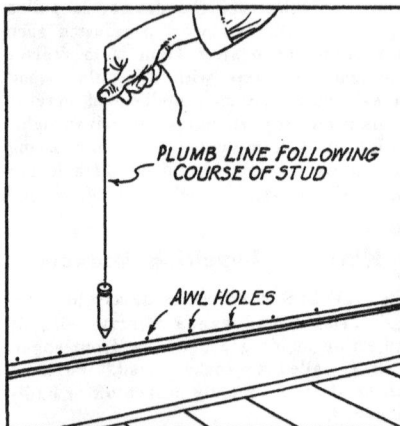

AWL STRIKING STUD

PLUMB LINE FOLLOWING COURSE OF STUD

AWL HOLES

Locating a stud is quite easy if a so-called "dowser" is available. It is an inexpensive tool designed for this very purpose. An experienced carpenter can detect the location fairly well by tapping the wall lightly with a hammer and judging by both the feel and the sound. Some craftsmen rely on a sensitive magnetic compass, which is deflected by the nails in the laths. The most certain method, however, is the one illustrated.

Take an ice pick or awl and drive small holes every inch through the wall, just above and very close to the baseboard. Because plaster laths are springy, it is best to make certain the studding has been located. As a test, use a hammer to drive the ice pick. The small holes can seldom be seen. After the studding is located, a plumb line can be used to locate the position of studding high above the baseboard where the hanger is to be installed, as shown in the second sketch.

Stretching Wire Screening

IT IS a difficult task for the average person to get screen wire on the frame with any degree of tension. One method that has proved highly satisfactory is shown in the sketch. After the old wire has been removed, lay two 2 x 4's which are about 6" longer than the screen frame across two sawhorses. Then lay two more 2 x 4's, about the width of the frame, across the first two pieces. Lay the screen frame on these, and with two C-clamps placed in the middle of the screen, put about a 1½″

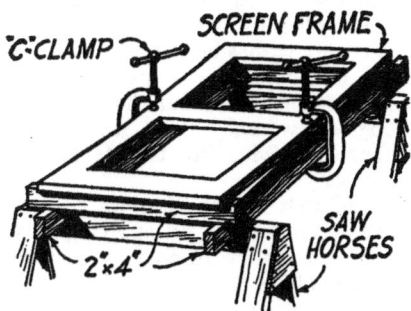

bow in the frame. Tack on the screen wire at both ends with a reasonable degree of tension, then release the C-clamps simultaneously, allowing the screen frame to go back to shape, thereby tightening the wire. The sides should then be fastened.

Prying Moldings from Plaster

WHEN doing alteration and repair work in old rooms, it often becomes necessary to pull nails or loosen moldings that have been fastened to the studding hidden behind plaster walls. In prying with a claw hammer or crowbar, unless proper care is taken, the plaster is broken and unsightly holes are left in the wall. These must be filled and painted later, and it is often a difficult task to make the paint match. To overcome this problem is a simple matter. Take a carpenter's saw, place the blade flat under the fulcrum of the hammer or bar, and pry. The steel saw blade distributes the pressure exerted at the fulcrum over so broad an area that the plaster will not crack or crumble.

Jack Aids in Removing Posts

WHEN deep-set wooden clothesline posts, gateposts or other posts have to be removed or relocated, it is difficult to raise them without a lot of laborious

spade work and some damage to the surrounding lawn. The easiest way is to use an auto jack. Nail a block on the post to take the thrust of the jack and another block high up on the opposite side so that a 2 x 4 can be used as a diagonal brace at the rear to keep the post from tipping backward under the pressure of the jack.

Drilling an Extra Deep Hole

WHEN a project in your home workshop calls for drilling an extra deep hole in wood, a length of stiff wire, slightly longer than the depth of the hole required,

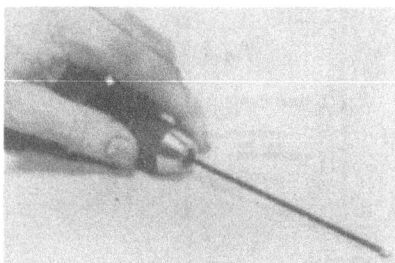

will finish the job nicely, after the hole has been drilled as far as possible in the ordinary way. The wire should be the same diameter as the drill, or a trifle smaller, and should be filed obliquely at the cutting end.

Wrench Helps Drive Staples

LARGE staples, such as those sometimes used for hasps on shed doors or gates, or even fence-wire staples are difficult to drive into oak or other hard wood. The legs of the staples are likely to spread

and bend under the weight of the hammer blows. To prevent this, grip the staple lightly with a thin adjustable wrench or a lever-jaw locking wrench as shown. This will help hold the staple in place and also prevent it from spreading.

Open Space at Baseboard Closed When Molding is Replaced Properly

WHEN floors in the home are being shellacked or waxed it is an appropriate time to remedy a condition, illustrated in Fig. A, which causes much annoyance to the housewife. The space that frequently shows up between the bottom of the baseboard and the floor can be eliminated without much effort. Quite often quarter-round molding is used to hide this crack, but if it has not been

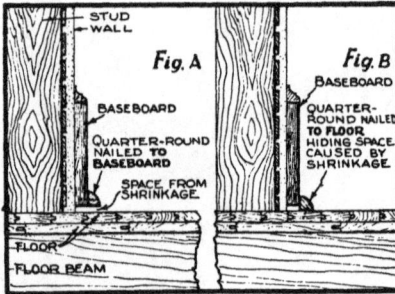

applied properly, it also will lift from the floor. It is an error when nailing this molding in place, to drive the nails into the baseboard. This procedure results in the molding lifting with the baseboard as the latter shrinks. The condition may be overcome if you will remove the molding and then nail it back in place by toeing the nails into the floor. See Fig. B. In this manner the molding is driven up tight to the baseboard but it will not interfere with the shrinkage of it.

Another error which may be found and should be avoided, is the nailing of molding to the floor and to the baseboard. The result will be that the quarter-round will split as shrinkage of the baseboard takes place. In construction where the studs rest on the sill and not on the floor beams this shrinkage is considerably greater due to the fact that the floor beams shrink down but do not carry the studs with them and the baseboard will then work up.

Water Will Usually Remove Marks And Scratches From Finished Work

HAMMER marks, dents and scratches on unfinished work cause the craftsman a great deal of trouble when the time comes to finish an article that has been made. Various types of fillers may be used to even out these blemishes but there is also a method whereby these faults may be corrected with little trouble and no expense.

It is well known that water will make wood swell. By applying this principle to the work an even surface may be obtained. The one thing that must be kept in mind is to apply the water to the indented portion of the wood only. An eye-dropper will serve the purpose in applying the water. Place a few drops on the blemish and allow it to soak into the wood. If the mark is not too deep the one application will be enough to bring the surface back to its original place. On the other hand should the indentation be too deep, it may be necessary to apply the water several times, allowing at least a half an hour between applications. In either case, let the wood stand over night after the last application. The surface may then be sanded down and it will be hard to find the blemish.

Needle in Small Bottle of Alcohol Makes a First Aid Kit for Slivers

NO WOODWORKER is immune to slivers. Regardless of how careful a person is when he handles rough lumber he will occasionally pick up a sliver in his hands.

The best insurance against infections from slivers is immediate removal, and this can be accomplished easily by keeping on hand in the workshop a one-ounce bottle of medicated alcohol in the cork of which is suspended a needle. The needle will always be handy and sterile. The cork at the end of it will furnish a grip.

Working Without a Helper

HOME owners sometimes have to handle long work without a helper. For example, it may be necessary to erect a long arbor, put in beams or joists for a new porch deck or floor, build an extension or the like.

One man, however, can accomplish a great deal by the judicious use of nails. If a beam or other horizontal member

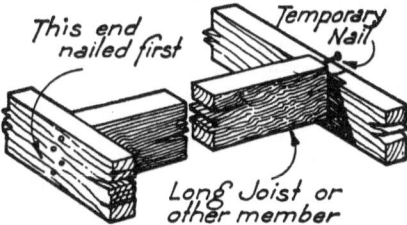

This end nailed first
Temporary Nail
Long Joist or other member

can't be held so that both ends may be nailed, it is often possible to support one end temporarily by driving one or more nails into the end at an angle as shown. This nail or nails may then be rested on some part already in place until the other end is secured. After that it is a simple matter to withdraw the temporary nails and complete the nailing. This is usually a good deal easier and safer than attempting to prop up such long members from below, where you are working.

Premature Sanding Dulls Tools

MANY a home craftsman who is relatively new at woodwork has ruined the cutting edge of his keen-edged tools by using sandpaper at the wrong time. A sanding operation, whether it be by hand at the bench, on the lathe, or on a power-driven sander, should not be done until after all tool work with cutting tools has been completed. Sanding deposits fine particles of grit in the pores of the wood, and should a keen-edged tool be used on such surfaces, the embedded grit will ruin the edge.

Prop Aids Wallboard Installation

WHEN wallboard is being applied to ceiling or wall, a tee-shaped prop will be extremely useful. The bar of the tee should be faced with canvas or rubber to protect the wallboard. Stock lumber 1″

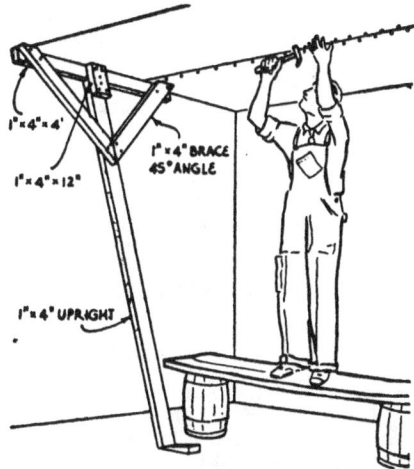

1″×4″×4′
1″×4″ BRACE 45° ANGLE
1″×4″×12″
1″×4″ UPRIGHT

x 4″ is used throughout; wood screws 1½″ long assemble the members.

With two of these props, each placed a foot from the ends, a large panel can be held securely against the ceiling beams while nails are driven to fasten the panel in place. When used to hold wallboard on a sidewall, a sack of dirt is used to brace the foot. When a person works alone on repair jobs, props like these help to hold things in place and may be adapted to many different types of jobs.

Two Ways to Remove Shingles

IN REPAIR work around old houses, it is sometimes necessary to remove wooden shingles without damaging them unneces-

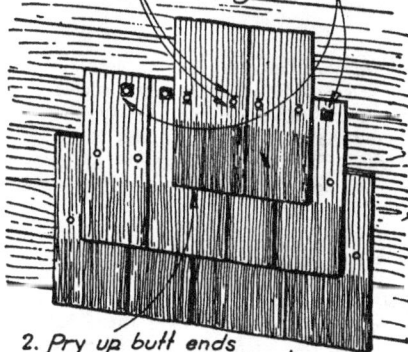

1. Cut above and below nailheads with narrow chisel
3. Withdraw the projecting nails
2. Pry up butt ends to remove shingles

sarily so that some of them can be replaced later. One method commonly used is to drive the nails right through the shingles with a nail set and hammer. In this case the nails are left in the sheathing or shingle laths.

A somewhat better way, however, is to use a sharp, narrow chisel to cut the shingles across the grain just above and below each nailhead as shown. A ¼" wood chisel is large enough for this purpose. The shingles can then be pried up easily and the projecting nails withdrawn.

Boring Holes in Wood Beads

OCCASIONS arise when the home craftsman is required to bore holes in wooden beads. Without the proper means for holding such a shape, it is almost impossible to do the job satisfactorily. A simple fixture and one that will prove surprisingly successful can be made of a piece of ¾" stock.

By cutting two V-grooves at right angles to one another as shown in the photo-

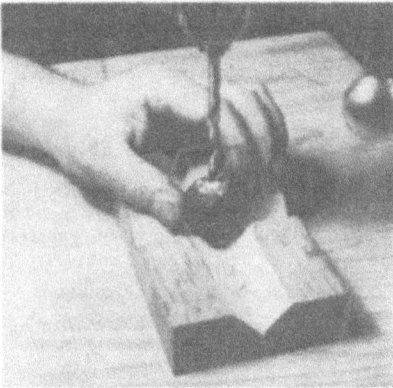

graph, then placing the wooden ball at the intersection of the grooves, a hole can be bored without difficulty. The grooves should be cut with their side at a 45° angle. This can be done on the bench saw by tilting the table or arbor to the required angle.

Wire Solder Has Many Uses

IN AN emergency, wire solder can be used for many purposes other than that for which it is intended. For example, an ordinary household tool kit rarely has a hand drill which will hold very fine drills such as are used in making inlaid pictures and other delicate jigsaw work, constructing models and the like. It is easy to hold a drill which may be .02" or even less in diameter by first inserting it into a short length of resin-core wire solder. The drill will penetrate the central hole through the solder without difficulty. When the solder is gripped in the drill chuck, it will be compressed to suit the shape of the jaws and will hold the drill securely.

Wire solder will also serve for template purposes. It can be readily bent around an odd-shaped profile and used to transfer the shape to drawing paper or the stock which is to be worked.

A very short rivet is sometimes required to secure a loose buckle to a belt or to repair some other leather article. If none is at hand, a short piece of wire solder may be used as a substitute. Punch a hole just large enough to receive the solder, insert the makeshift rivet and hammer the ends flat.

When wood screws work loose and screws of heavier gauge are not on hand, it is often more convenient to plug the holes with bits of wire solder than to use plugs of wood, steel wool or hole-filling cement.

Removing Jar Tops

CAPS on shellac jars and on other types of screw-cap jars are often difficult to remove after they have been stored for an extended period. A sheet of sandpaper placed over the lid, with the abrasive side in contact with the metal as shown in the photo, will provide a firm grip that will usually loosen the lid. For especially tight lids, the jar top may have to be dipped in hot water before it can be unscrewed.

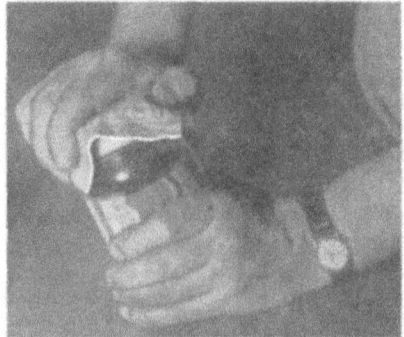

Lubricating with Graphite

GRAPHITE in stick or powder form has many uses around the shop and home. It is a desirable substitute for oil and grease in many applications where the latter have a tendency to stain or become gummy with grit and dirt.

For example, the tailstock center of a wood-turning lathe can be lubricated with graphite to advantage. Oil, especially if too freely applied, penetrates the wood deeply and spreads, which is sometimes objectionable.

Vises, C-clamps, hand screws, lathe chucks, bench-saw tilting and raising mechanisms, jigsaw blade guides and similar parts may be lubricated with graphite. It is also excellent for locks, hinges and hardware of various types. The powdered variety of graphite, which is usually sold in a small plastic applicator, can be blown into holes and crevices where it would be difficult to apply oil successfully without having it drip or run over adjacent surfaces where not wanted.

Envelope Serves As Funnel

THE need for a small funnel arises many times in the shop and around the house to transfer liquids and powders. In most instances the household funnel belongs in the kitchen and cannot be used for transferring such materials as linseed oil, alcohol, paint and powdered stains.

An excellent substitute for a small funnel, and one that does not require cleaning after use, is a discarded envelope. An envelope is converted into a funnel by cutting off a small corner on the closed end and using as shown in the sketch.

Preventing Rust in the Shop

RUST is an enemy the home craftsman has to fight constantly. No craftsman who takes pride in his equipment likes to see the unprotected surfaces of power tools and other equipment become rusty or tarnished, yet it is difficult to prevent this in damp weather or in climates where the humidity is often high. Going over the machines with an oily rag at frequent intervals will help, but a more permanent method of protecting surfaces that are not subject to wear is to clean them thoroughly, then apply a coat of clear metal lacquer or well-thinned white shellac.

Lubricating Planes and Saws

A LITTLE lubrication makes sawing and planing considerably easier. It is a good idea to fasten a felt pad to a block of convenient size and moisten it with lard oil or other suitable lubricant. Rub the pad over the bottom of planes and on the sides of handsaws before using them. You will be surprised at how much less muscle the work seems to require. Circular and band saws can be similarly treated, particularly when sawing very tough, resinous or especially thick stock.

Sprinkling Abrasive Powders

POWDERED pumice stone, rottenstone, emery and other abrasive and polishing agents in powder form can be more conveniently used if kept, properly labeled, in cheap, large, restaurant-type salt shakers. It is then easier to sprinkle the powder evenly over the surface that is to be rubbed down or polished. This is also true when the abrasive is applied for some other purpose, as when fine emery flour is sprinkled on a leather strop to improve its "bite."

If large surfaces, such as table, desk or chest tops, have to be given a rubbed finish, it is still better to get a low-priced kitchen flour sifter. This will spread an even layer of pumice stone in next to no time. The powder is then rubbed with a hard piece of rubbing felt at least ½" thick. The felt is first dipped in water or oil, depending upon whether an oil or water rub is being used. The even distribution of the powder helps in obtaining a uniform finish and lessens the amount of spot rubbing which otherwise would have to be done.

Tape Keeps Fingers from Being Cut

SMALL squares of adhesive tape serve to protect a worker's fingers from abrasions and cuts caused by handling sharp or rough objects. Short strips of tape are applied to the thumb, forefinger and second finger. For jobs requiring finger dexterity, gloves are not very practical. The tape trick works better.

Remove Pitch from Saw Blade

CIRCULAR saw blades that are used for cutting woods containing a considerable quantity of pitch have the gullets and sides of the teeth filled with sawdust that adheres tenaciously to the metal. Using a saw blade in this condition not only results in overloading the motor, but may be the cause of a burned blade. The pitch and hardened sawdust can be removed readily by immersing the blade in a container of solvent that will loosen the pitch. Such solvents as turpentine or kerosene will be found satisfactory. Allow the blade to remain in the liquid for at least 12 hours; then when the sawdust has softened, it can be removed with a brush. If the first treatment is not sufficient, repeat.

Shop Uses for Scotch Tape

TRANSPARENT cellulose tape, or Scotch tape as it is commonly called, is useful for many shop purposes. It pays to keep three or four rolls of different widths on hand.

Labels. To apply labels indicating the contents of drawers, jars, bottles and cans, use this tape. Type or print the label on paper, then take a piece of Scotch tape slightly wider than the width of the label and cut it an inch longer. Hold the ends of the tape and let only the center of it come in contact with the center of the label. Lift the label, set it in position and press it into contact, working from the center to the ends. When the contents are changed, it is necessary only to peel off the tape and apply a new label in the same way.

Matching Veneers. If you do much matching of small pieces of veneer, the tape is again of help. Use it on the face of the veneer in place of the usual paper veneer tape. Its transparency permits a full view of the matching job, and when the veneer is in place it is an easy matter to peel off the tape. If it has been in place for a long time, some of the sticky substance may adhere to the veneer, but this can be wiped off with turpentine or benzine.

Marquetry. Do you do much marquetry? If so, use the tape for holding the pieces together. This eliminates a couple of steps and is easier than the old way of first gluing down the pieces with mucilage and later gluing paper over the face, then attaching to the core stock and removing the face paper after the glue has set. When the tape is used, the pieces are matched to the master drawing, held with tape over the face and glued to the core. The tape is peeled off when glue has dried.

Maker's Name on Furniture

SOME amateur cabinetmakers are turning out furniture today that is equal in quality of workmanship, design and finish to the best custom-made pieces. Articles of furniture of this type are likely to become family heirlooms and far outlast the memory of who made them or when. For this reason it is advisable for the builder to sign or letter his name and add the date in some hidden place, such as inside the apron or under the top of a table or inside one of the seat rails of a chair.

Floor Sandpaper for Disks

MOST people in the floor sanding business have paper that has been so damaged or torn at the edges that it is useless to them. This paper is usually of high quality and can be cut and used on an 8" or 9" disc sander. The paper is generally 8" wide, which makes it right for 8" disks; however, it can be used nicely on a 9" disk by cementing on a strip to build the disk up to 9". Contact your neighborhood floor sander and see if he isn't willing to let you have his damaged or worn paper.

PART 4
Better Work-Holding Ideas

M OST amateur woodworkers—and a good many professionals, too— could save themselves a good deal of effort by making better use of the hand screw. It has been called the "tool of a thousand uses" and the "woodworker's third hand." Both phrases are well deserved.

Whenever you have difficulty in holding something, think of the hand screw. This goes far beyond the ordinary clamping of glue joints.

For example, if you have to do some work away from your workshop, you can rig up a substitute for a woodworking vise with the aid of two good-sized hand screws. Lay one of them flat on any available table with one jaw projecting over the edge and hold it in place with another hand screw.

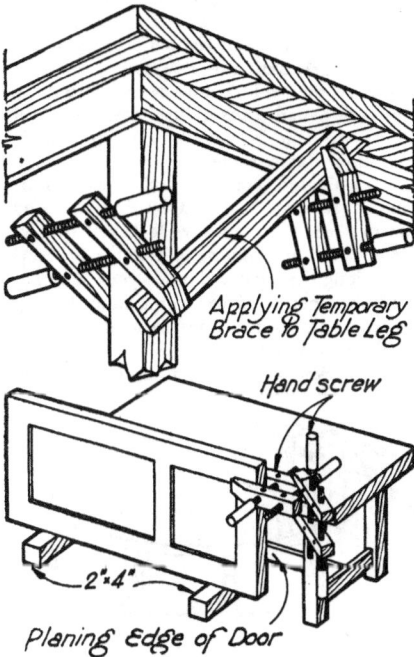

Bar Clamp

Hand screw

Door Stile

Door Rail

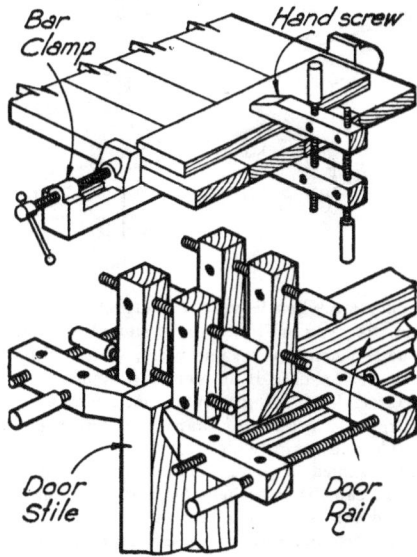

Applying Temporary Brace to Table Leg

Hand screw

2"x4"

Planing Edge of Door

This substitute vise is excellent for holding doors or large panels for planing the edges. If the table is shaky, use a scrap piece of 2 x 4 or other wood as a brace, running it from the left end of the table down to the junction of floor and wall.

Even when you are working at a regular bench, a hand screw is valuable for supporting the right end of long boards, panels and frames. Clamp the hand screw on the work at a convenient height and let it rest on the bench top while the outer end of the work is held in the vise. Some carpenter's benches have a series of holes bored through the apron so that a pin can be inserted to support the loose end of a long board, but the hand-screw method is adapted to a greater variety of work of all widths.

When narrow boards are being glued together with bar clamps to form a wide

73

board or panel, it is common practice, of course, to clamp on one or more strips of wood across the grain with hand screws to prevent the work from buckling. Often a strip is put across both top and bottom of the panel to hold it perfectly flat.

Although not so well known, it is equally good practice to use hand screws and strips of wood to clamp any thin, flat work to the

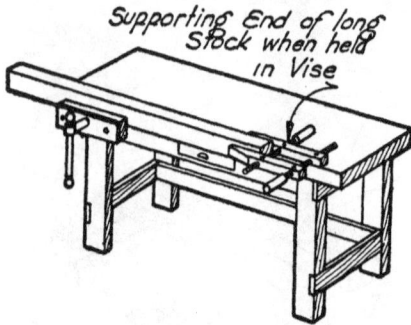

Supporting End of long Stock when held in Vise

bench top when leaving it overnight. If you do that, you will find the material in good shape when you resume work, which might not be the case if it were left unclamped. Material left lying around, not under pressure, may get out of shape in a few hours.

Curved work which cannot conveniently be clamped with bar clamps for gluing a joint can often be held by first fastening a hand screw to each section near the joint and then drawing the parts together with other hand screws or bar clamps which are tightened against the hand screws that were first attached.

Sometimes when working with certain woods, especially those that are highly figured or have irregular grain, a small section will lift up. Touch a spot of glue under the sliver, place a piece of old paper and a block of wood on top, and apply a hand screw. This will repair the surface in short order, especially if a fast-setting glue such as the new type of polyvinyl resin glue is used.

In planing or scraping thin material against a bench stop, the wood may be inclined to buckle. In this case, hold down the rear end with a hand screw. Reverse the stock in order to clean up the last few inches which were covered by the hand screw during the operation.

When preparing thin panels which are to slide into grooves in a framework, take the precaution to pile up the panels, as they are finished, with strips of wood placed across

the grain between them. Hold the pile flat with hand screws. Then, when you are ready to insert the panels into the grooves of the framework, they will go in readily, having been kept flat.

Time can be saved when cleaning out mortises, coping or doing other work on the ends of rails if a number of the rails are placed on the bench top at once and held

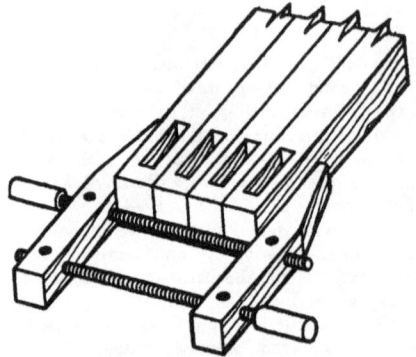

together with a hand screw at each end. This is faster than holding each piece separately in the vise.

To prevent thin wood from splitting when you are boring holes near the end, clamp on a hand screw. If a split does start, apply glue and tighten a hand screw on the work until the glue sets. An open crack at the end should be filled with a wedged-shaped piece of the same wood cut so it will slip in without forcing. Apply glue and clamp as before.

A laminated arch and other curved or bent work may be glued by first drawing the desired curve on a wide board or plywood panel and nailing triangular brackets to it along the curved line. If your shop has a wooden floor and you don't mind driving nails into it, the floor may be used for large work. Cut a notch in the slanting edge of each bracket so the hand screws will not

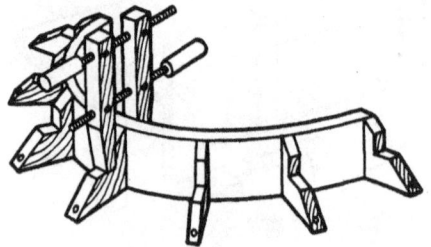

slip. Then the stock, whether thin wood, veneer or a saw-kerfed board, can be bent against the vertical edges of the brackets and held with hand screws.

Hand screws can also often be used to advantage when fitting trim, long moldings and the like, especially if the work is irregular or curved. Fit one end first and fasten it in place with a hand screw while marking the other end.

The more you accustom yourself to using hand screws, the more uses you will find for them and the easier it will be to accomplish otherwise difficult jobs.

Setting Hand Screws Quickly

HAND screws are used so frequently in cabinetmaking and other woodworking that it pays to learn to handle them speedily and without waste motions.

The best trick is to make a habit of always holding a hand screw as shown in Fig. 1 when swinging them to open or close the jaws to the approximate opening required. Note that the left hand grasps the middle spindle, and the right hand holds the end or outer spindle. The handles are held firmly and the jaws revolved around the spindles with a swinging motion. Swinging the jaws inward towards the face will open them; in the other direction, close them. This quickly becomes auto-

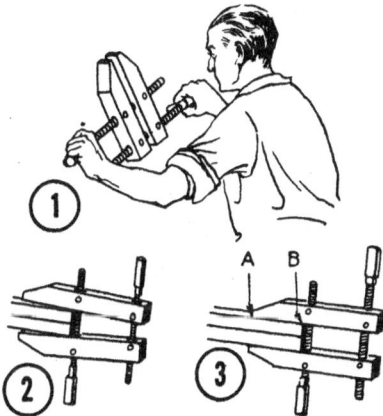

matic, provided you always hold the hand screws as just described. If, however, you pick them up at random, sometimes with the middle spindle in the left hand and sometimes in the right, you always have to make a tentative swing in order to see whether the jaws are opening or closing.

In placing a hand screw on the work, the left hand goes underneath and the right hand above, leaving the hand screw as shown in Fig. 2. On vertical work, of course, the right hand will go to the right and the left hand to the left. This leaves the spindles in a natural position so that the end spindle is always turned to the right to tighten the jaws.

Place the hand screw so that the middle spindle is as close to the work as possible. Then adjust one or both spindles so that the hand screw grips the edge of the work easily while the points of the jaws are slightly open, as in Fig. 2. The middle spindle ordinarily requires no further adjustment. The jaws are now tightened by turning the end spindle until they grip the work uniformly from A to B, Fig. 3.

To be sure the pressure is even, try moving the jaws from side to side. If they do move, tighten the end spindle still more, using both hands if necessary.

Oiled Hand Screws Shed Glue

HAND screws that are used to hold stock being glued together frequently become covered with excess glue forced from the joints. This glue is extremely difficult to remove from the surfaces of the hand screws after the glue has set. One method of protecting these surfaces from having the glue adhere to them is to apply a coat of warm linseed oil. The function of the linseed oil is to close the pores and to produce an oily surface to which it is impossible for the glue to stick.

Oil of this type should be heated in a double boiler. The oil is placed in the upper section of the boiler and hot water in the lower section. Under no condition is it safe to place a container of linseed oil over or near an open flame. There is always the danger of overheating the oil and causing a fire.

The warm oil is applied to the surfaces of the clamp with a brush. Several applications at intervals of four hours will result in a surface impervious to glue.

Clamp Holds Odd-Shaped Work

SIX SIDED, eight-sided and other odd-shaped work is difficult to clamp up when gluing unless special flexible clamps are available. However, a substitute for them can be improvised from two blocks of wood, a short dowel and a length of

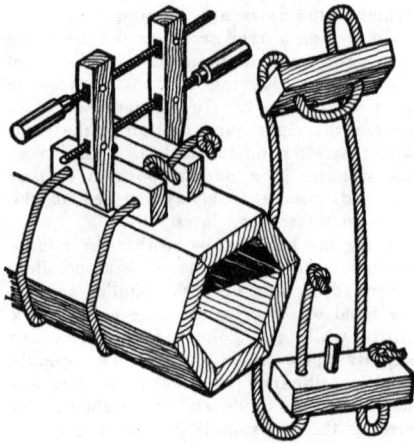

sash cord or other strong, nonstretching rope.

Two holes are bored through each block as indicated to take the rope, and the dowel is glued in one of the blocks close to one or the other of the holes. The rope is then threaded through the holes and a knot tied in each end.

In use, the rope is adjusted around the work as tightly as possible and the loose end is fastened by carrying it around the pin and back under itself. The blocks are then drawn together with a hand screw or large C-clamp.

Spring Clamps Have Many Uses

SPRING clamps save much time in many small woodworking operations and repair jobs, not to speak of model making and various special types of craftwork.

The most powerful and generally useful type of spring clamp is that shown in Fig. 1, where it is being used to hold a veneer patch while the glue sets. This clamp can be obtained from craftwork supply houses and well-stocked hardware stores. A 6″ clamp of this kind will open to about 2″ wide and exert considerable pressure—sufficient for many minor gluing operations. It is particularly valuable

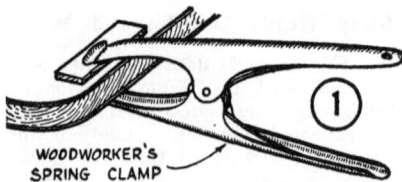

WOODWORKER'S SPRING CLAMP

when patching veneered work, gluing down small slivers of wood and holding a number of pieces of veneer together temporarily, as when preparing a "book" of veneers for making an inlaid picture.

For smaller work, spring clamps like those shown in Fig. 2 are useful. They

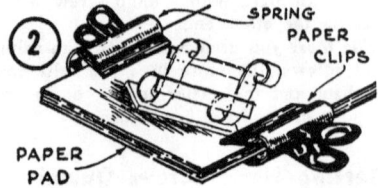

SPRING PAPER CLIPS

PAPER PAD

come in various sizes, are cheap in price and can be obtained in stationery stores and at the stationery counters of chain stores. For some work it is desirable to bend the jaws slightly to distribute their pressure over a larger area of the work, particularly if very thin material is to be held. Such clamps are frequently used for difficult trimming and gluing operations where nothing else would serve the purpose as well; for example, holding pieces of turkey feather that are to be prepared for gluing to arrow shafts.

The least expensive clamps of all—so cheap, in fact, that they can be regarded as expendable—are spring-clip wooden clothespins (Fig. 3). For very small work these are excellent. The jaws can quickly be whittled or filed to any shape necessary;

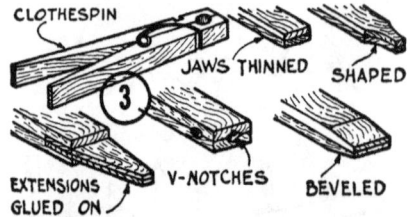

CLOTHESPIN

JAWS THINNED   SHAPED

EXTENSIONS GLUED ON   V-NOTCHES   BEVELED

notches can be filed into them for round or odd-shaped work; strips of wood can be glued on to make extension jaws for very special, delicate jobs; and the spring pressure can be increased simply by wrapping a heavy rubber band around the jaws.

Equipped with an assortment of these three types of clamps, the home craftsman is in a position to cope with any small clamping jobs, no matter how complicated.

Improper Application of Bar Clamps Throws work out of Square

THE use of bar clamps is almost an absolute necessity when constructing pieces of furniture. At first appearance it would seem that there is nothing difficult to the handling of this piece of shop equipment but as many home craftsmen may have discovered, a great deal of trouble may be encountered if these are not applied properly. In the gluing up of work such as a table or a box the clamps hold the work together until the glue has set. The danger, at this

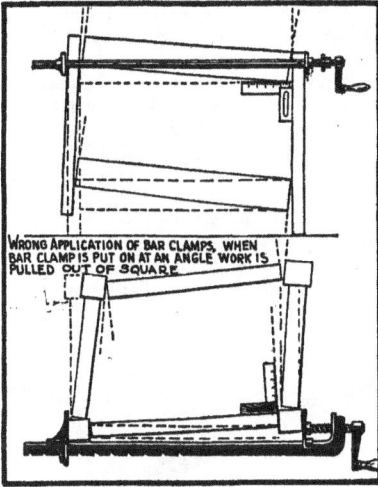

WRONG APPLICATION OF BAR CLAMPS, WHEN BAR CLAMP IS PUT ON AT AN ANGLE WORK IS PULLED OUT OF SQUARE

point, lies in throwing the assembled work out of square when pressure is applied by the clamps. This trouble is caused entirely by the improper application of the clamps and may be remedied quickly and easily provided the craftsman knows what to do.

The first sketch shows a table end in the clamps. The drawing is exaggerated slightly in order to bring out the various points to be discussed. It shows the clamp, high on one leg and low on the other. The result of this is obvious; the assembly is out of square and the shoulders of the rails do not meet flush with the legs. It can be corrected by raising the end of the clamp which is low so

that the bar will be parallel to the edge of the rail.

The second sketch shows the clamp from a different view. Here as before, the clamp as applied is pulling the assembly out of square. The changing of the clamp as described in the first instance, will not correct the error as shown in this sketch. In this case the cause is the result of not having the clamp parallel to the face of the rail. The correction is nothing more than shifting the clamp to the proper position in relation to the rail. If these errors and corrections are kept in mind, it will not be necessary to use temporary diagonal braces to keep the work square.

Bar Clamp Blocks Leave Hands Free

When wide panels that are awkward to handle are being set up in clamps after being glued, it is convenient to

have the clamps held in a fixed position. Small wood blocks cut from 2 x 4 stock slotted and nailed to a base do the trick.

Clamping Picture Moldings

COMMERCIAL picture frames are so expensive that many home craftsmen make their own, especially as high-grade finished and semifinished moldings can readily be obtained in small quantities from craftwork supply houses. There is little difficulty in making frames, provided an accurate miter box and a sharp back saw are available. The main problem arises in clamping the joints while they are being glued and nailed or, in certain cases, screwed.

The most convenient method of clamping is, of course, to use a regular picture frame vise or miter vise as it is usually called. This type of vise ordinarily clamps any

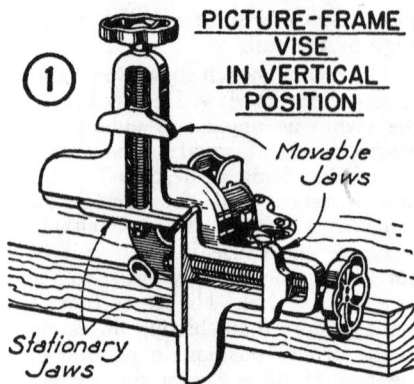

PICTURE-FRAME VISE IN VERTICAL POSITION

Movable Jaws

Stationary Jaws

type of picture molding up to about 4" wide. It is often used in a horizontal position, but for greater convenience in nailing may be turned to a vertical position as shown in Fig. 1. The stationary jaws fit into the picture rabbet and the movable jaws press against the outside edge of the molding. If many frames are to be made, buy a vise of this kind to save time and insure square, accurate joints.

When only a few frames are to be made, a jig for holding the joints can easily be

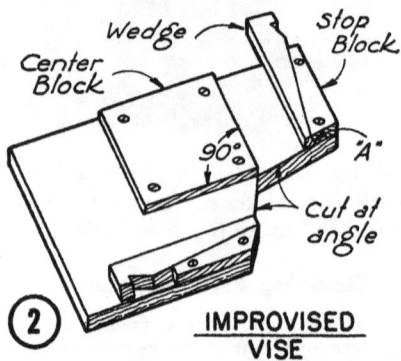

Wedge

Center Block

Stop Block

90°

"A"

Cut at angle

IMPROVISED VISE

devised. These may be made in many ways, but a simple form which approximates the commercial vise in the method of operation is shown in Fig. 2. It may be made from scraps of wood in any size according to the moldings to be used.

The discarded end of an 8", 10" or 12" board at least ¾" thick will make a satisfactory base provided it is not warped, or a waste piece of thick plywood will do equally well. To serve the same purpose as the stationary jaws of the commercial vise, a square piece of wood or plywood

⅜" thick is attached to the base. The clamping edges must be perfectly square and form an exact right angle as the squareness of the frames depends upon this detail. Make this piece as large as the dimensions of the baseboard permit, following roughly the proportions in Fig. 2.

One corner of the baseboard is now cut away and the cuts are angled slightly as shown to meet the corner of the center block. The purpose is to give more space when nailing frame members together.

Two pair of wedges and stop blocks ¾" thick are then prepared. When cutting these, it is best to use a compound angle as indicated at A so that the wedge will be held down by the block, the effect being something like that of a dovetail slide The blocks are fastened to the baseboard with screws. They may be placed permanently as shown, in which case wedges of various widths will have to be made to take care of moldings of different sizes, or the blocks can be shifted as necessary and the one pair of wedges used. If the ends of the wedges are found to project too far into the corner space, where they would interfere with nailing, simply cut them off or move the blocks in closer.

This improvised clamp may be used in a horizontal position, but unlike most home-

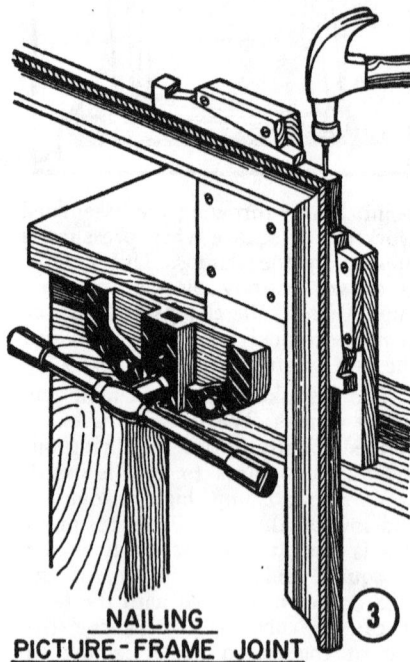

NAILING PICTURE-FRAME JOINT

made picture-frame vises, it can also be held vertical, which makes nailing easier. Usually it can be held in the regular woodworking vise as shown in Fig. 3, but if the size of the frame is such that the vise interferes, the work can be done flat or the clamp may be fastened to the edge of the workbench with screws or C-clamps.

Since glue may be squeezed out on the clamp, the parts which come in contact with the joints should be well waxed or .oiled, or a piece of wax paper should be placed between moldings and clamp.

In using any kind of picture-frame vise, great pains must be taken that the movable jaws or wedges do not damage the outer edge of the molding. Finished moldings must be handled with the utmost care. Thin pieces of soft wood or strips of cardboard may be used to pad the moldings when they are placed in the vise.

It is well to drill lead holes before driving nails, thus removing any danger that· the wood will split, and lessening the likelihood, in the case of a homemade clamp, that the wedges will be jarred loose.

Jack Holds Door for Planing

HOME owners sometimes have difficulty in planing the edges of a door which fits too tight or in fitting a new door, storm door or screen door. To make this work easier, it takes only a few minutes to nail together a stand or jack to hold the door.

The jack is made as shown from two heavy blocks, such as waste ends cut from a 2 x 6. These are nailed to a piece of thin wood or lath with sufficient space between so that the door will rest in the notch thus formed with hardly any clearance. Two strips are then nailed under the jack to form feet. The lower edge of the door is placed between the jaws

DOOR FITS SNUGLY BETWEEN JAWS

DOOR JACK

of the jack, and the weight on the somewhat springy cross strip causes the jaws to grip the door securely.

Plane the lock edge of the door first, using the longest plane available. Be sure to get it perfectly straight, and bevel it slightly toward the side which is to go against the door stop. Next, prop the door in place with the lock edge against the jamb and have an assistant, if possible, mark the correct width by drawing a pencil along the other jamb. If the surplus wood is $\frac{1}{4}''$ or more, cut it off with a rip saw before planing this edge; otherwise, place the door back in the jack with the hinge edge uppermost and plane down to the line.

The jack is also useful in holding the door while cutting hinge and lock mortises.

Holding Awkward Work in Vise

WHEN a long, irregularly shaped piece of wood cannot be held securely in the vise, yet it is necessary to chisel a recess in it or do other shaping, planing or boring operations, the work can

often be done by using the expedient illustrated. A cabinetmaker's bar clamp is first placed in the vise; then the awkwardly shaped piece of wood is secured in the clamp. In this instance, a section of molded birch handrail required two notches to be cut into the underside.

Linoleum Makes Vise-Jaw Pads

IN CERTAIN types of work it is desirable to pad the jaws of a bench vise so that the part being gripped will not be bruised or scratched. Good pads for this purpose can be cut from scrap pieces of heavy linoleum. If cut to fit the vise properly, they will stay in place fairly well by themselves, but they can be cemented to the jaws if preferred.

PART 5
Power-Tool Hints

THE JOB of gluing two or more boards together to produce a wide panel is required of every craftsman who constructs furniture. The most common method of doing this work is by use of dowels. A good dowel joint can be made only with the greatest of care in locating the dowel holes in the edges of the joining pieces and in boring the holes to have them square with the edge. A tongue-and-groove joint·is also used, but it requires two set-ups on the saw. A more satisfactory glue joint can be made through the use of a special cutter which can be fitted on the bench saw arbor. A single-cutter shapes the edges of both members being joined. The joint formed by this cutter increases the area of the butting edges and thereby increases the strength of the joint.

The cutter illustrated can be used on stock ranging in thickness from $\frac{5}{8}''$ to 2''.

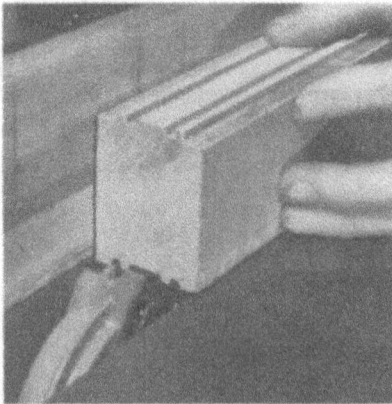

It is placed on the saw arbor and the table is adjusted so that the working surface of the table lines up with the cutter as shown in Fig. 1. The rip fence is set

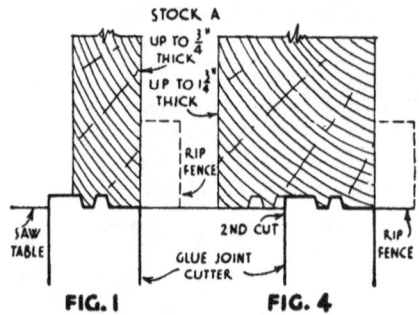

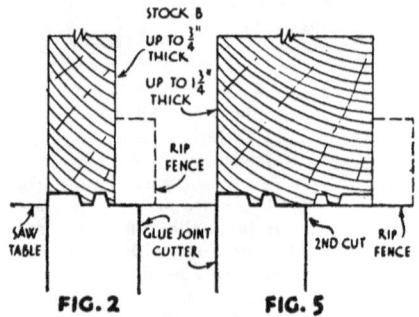

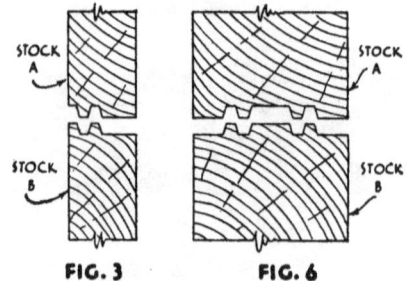

FIG. 1

FIG. 2

FIG. 3

FIG. 4

FIG. 5

FIG. 6

so that the first piece of stock to be cut (A) lines up with the right side of the cutter as shown in Fig. 1. After the piece has been passed over the cutter it has the shape of (A) as shown in Fig. 3. The second piece (B) is cut by setting the rip fence so that the stock will line up with the left side of the cutter as shown in Fig. 2. This piece has the reverse cut of (A). The pieces fit together as shown in Fig. 3.

Stock ranging from $1\frac{3}{4}''$ to $2''$ is cut by setting the fence in the same manner as already described, but in this case the stock is passed over the cutter first with one face against the fence and then with the other face against the fence. The result will be a cut having the contour as shown in Figs. 4 and 5. The two pieces will fit together as shown in Fig. 6.

Stock ranging between $1''$ and $1\frac{3}{4}''$ in thickness can be cut as already described for wider stock with the exception that when the same piece of stock is passed over the cutter to make the second cut, the fence will have to be reset.

Cutting Stopped Dadoes

IN panel construction it is very often necessary to cut dadoes so as not to have the opening carry through to the end of the stock. The general practice is to set up the saw, then let the stock come down on the dado head at the point the dado is to start. After the stock has had a small cut in it, the piece is removed from the saw and inspected to see if the cut was started at the right point. If it has not been cut correctly, it must be placed on the saw again. This time the stock is moved back a little to get the correct location. This same procedure of trial and error must be resorted to when the end of the dado cut has been reached. The method is very annoying and wastes considerable time if a number of like pieces are to be cut.

A simpler method, and by far a more accurate one, may be used to do this work. Obtain a piece of wood, $\frac{3}{4}''$ x $2\frac{1}{2}''$ and about twice as long as your piece of stock that is to be grooved. Fasten this piece to the fence of the saw with a couple of screws, in such a manner as to have as much of it in front of the saw as there is behind it. Set the fence

CUTTING STOP DADOES

for the distance between the dado and the inside of the work, then set the dado head to the depth of cut required. Mark the length of the dado on the work; that is, mark where it should start and stop. Place the work alongside of the saw so as to line up the beginning of the cut with the teeth on the far side. The end of the work toward you will be projecting beyond the table and where this end comes, fasten a hand screw to the piece of wood that has been attached to the fence. This clamp will form a guide for starting the cut.

Now move the stock down so as to have the end of the dado cut come in line with the forward tooth of the saw. At this point on the auxiliary fence apply a second hand screw which will form the second stop for the dado cut. The saw is then started and the back end of the wood is placed against the first stop. The stock is let down over the dado head, then is pushed forward until the end strikes the second stop. The result will be a dado that has really started and stopped exactly where you wanted it. Any number of like pieces may be cut without fear of having the dadoes too long or too short.

Tenoning Fixture for Saw

BY USING this husky tenoning fixture, you can be sure many operations will be quick and accurate and also safer. The fixture is invaluable when end ripping boards on the circular saw, but you can

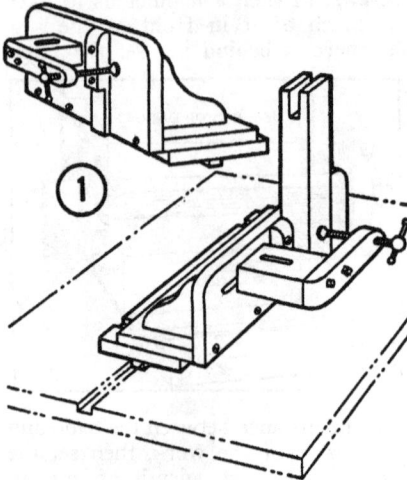

also use it to great advantage on the shaper when grooving the face of narrow stock. The unit is guided by a spline sliding in the table groove, and when you advance the work into the saw or cutters, your hands are kept a safe distance away. The work is held in position as in Fig. 1 by a convenient clamp that is adjustable for many kinds of work.

Dimensions for the tenoning fixture are given in Fig. 2. The face member is fastened to the sub-base with screws and well braced with two blocks. This unit slides crosswise over the base and is held in alignment by two guides.

The bracket can be made conveniently from a piece of 2x4. A ¼" carriage bolt and wing nut holds the bracket against the face. It will be necessary to cut a slot through the bracket to permit the insertion of this bolt. The slot in the face permits you to shift the bracket as required to place the clamp in the middle of the work. Make the arm of maple and fasten it securely to the bracket with lag screws.

The type of press screw sold for making veneer presses can be used for the clamping screw and is easily installed. If you have an old C-clamp, the screw from it will also work well. Take off the foot and remove the screw from the frame. Work

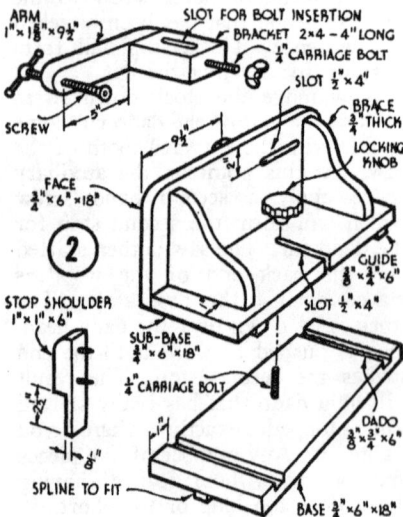

the screw into an undersize hole drilled in the arm and replace the foot. Should it be impossible to remove the foot, it will be necessary to saw the frame away from the screw. In this case, make the arm from two pieces as shown in Fig. 3. These pieces are clamped together and drilled undersize for the screw. Next remove the clamps, place the screw between the blocks and slowly squeeze them together again while turning the screw back and forth. After threads are made, the blocks are fastened together to form a solid arm. When attaching the stop shoulder to the face, note that the screws are in the upper part only. This will prevent damaging the saw should you accidentally run it into the shoulder.

Finally, add the spline, making sure it is parallel to the face.

• • •

Be sure to use a highly polished drill for plastics; the chips will twist out more readily. That's why even the flutes of special production drills for use in plastics are given a mirror finish.

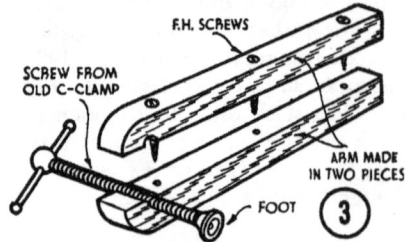

Sling Supports Long Board

WHEN crosscutting long, narrow pieces of stock on the bench saw, supporting the free end of the stock is often a problem. A simple remedy consists of suspending a rope sling from the ceiling directly over the free end of the stock and adjusting the sling to support the wood at sawtable height.

Saber Sawing on the Jig Saw

THERE are without question more jig saws in use throughout the country today than there are of any other two woodworking machines, yet a great many of the users do not realize that most of the jig saws (with the exception of the magnetic and rocker-arm type machines) can be used for saber sawing.

Saber sawing is becoming so popular that some manufacturers are now building saber saw machines. Most of these machines are designed to do filing as well as saber sawing. One of these machines is illustrated in operation, sawing out block letters from $\frac{1}{8}''$ Masonite.

In setting up a jig saw for inside sawing in scrollwork, it is necessary to release the saw blade at both ends, insert the blade through the material being sawed, set the blade back in the machine and tighten both ends before sawing. Any inside sawing where there are a lot of separate sections to saw out requires this operation to be repeated many times.

To convert the jig saw to a saber saw, simply push the saw-blade guide arm up as far as it will go, to make room for the work. Insert a saber saw blade (teeth down) in the clamp and drive head, just as you would the lower end of the jigsaw blade, and you are ready to do saber sawing.

Since the teeth of the saw are pointed down, the cutting is done on the down stroke; and simply by drilling a hole through the piece to be sawed out, setting the piece down over the saw blade, and starting the machine, the operation is started. When the section has been sawed out, stop the machine, lift the piece off, and proceed with other sections.

Sanding and Filing on Jig Saw

USING the jig saw for sanding and filing is something almost every craftsman has tried, but few realize the importance that speed has to the relation of efficiency and perfection. The speed at which a sanding drum or file operates in a jig saw should be low. If the sander is operated at a stepped-up speed, the result will be a glazing of the coated abrasive. Operating a file at a high speed will simply scrape the work without smoothing it.

Files that are designed for use on the jig saw are cut so that they do their work on the down stroke. This is different from the cut of a hand file which, if placed in the jig saw with the tang in the lower chuck, will cut on the upstroke. It is possible to use a hand file in the jig saw by inserting the point of the file in the lower chuck and the tang in the upper one. With the hand file inserted in this manner, it will cut on the down stroke.

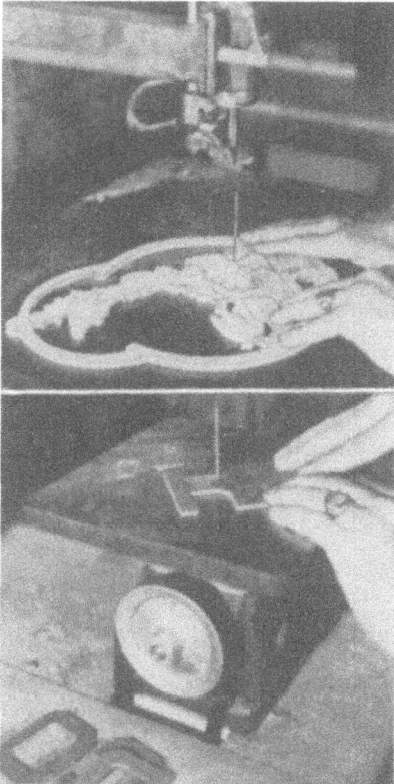

Cutting Panels on Bench Saw

PLYWOOD and various types of wallboards come in standard four-foot widths and often prove difficult to rip on the bench saw. If your saw fence will accommodate a setting of 24" from the blade, you can easily cut any width panel desired. If you wish to rip a width greater than 24", compute the remainder of the 4-ft. panel above the width required, subtract the thickness of the kerf made by the saw blade and set the fence to that dimension. For instance, a 38" panel may be ripped from a standard 48" sheet by setting the rip fence 10" from the outside of the saw blade.

Planer Saws Need to Project

AMATEUR woodworkers frequently have difficulty with hollow- or concave-ground circular saws, which are commonly called planer saws because they cut so smoothly. These saws often seem to work so hard that the friction causes excessive heat or burning. For this the blade itself is likely to be blamed. Actually, the trouble usually lies in the way the blade is adjusted.

Unlike ordinary circular saws, a hollow-ground blade should project through the cut as far as practicable, as shown at A in the accompanying illustration. If the saw is adjusted so that the teeth barely clear the stock, as at B, too much of the thick rim of the saw is running in the cut. Little or no advantage is then gained from the hollow-ground feature of the blade, which is its most important characteristic.

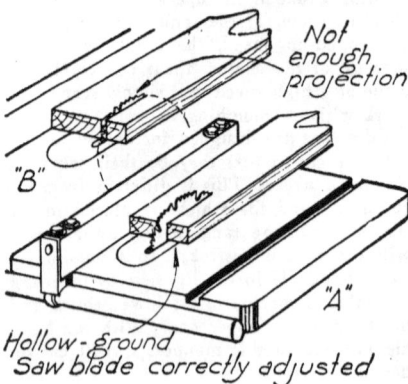

Not enough projection

"B"

Hollow-ground Saw blade correctly adjusted

"A"

Without the clearance obtained by this feature, the saw is almost certain to heat up, as the teeth themselves are not set to cut sufficient clearance.

Cutting Wide Panels on Saw

YOU can cut panels of almost any size in any direction on a bench saw by the following simple method:

Rip a strip $\frac{3}{8}$" thick from the edge of a $\frac{3}{4}$" board. The strip should be at least one foot longer than the cut to be made. If the strip is over $\frac{3}{8}$" thick, rip the piece again or plane it until it slides freely in the saw-table groove. Locate this strip on the back of the work, either square or at the angle of the cut to be made. Let it project a foot on the entering side of the cut. Fasten the strip to the work with a few brads. Enter the strip in the saw-table slot and it will guide the work into the blade. If you have much of this kind of work to do, make the strip of hard wood.

Figuring Angle Cuts on Bench Saw

THE cutting of stock at an angle on the bench saw by tilting table or blade often confuses the craftsman when the angle to be cut is not within the range of 45° to 90°. Most bench saws have a quadrant marked in degrees from 45 to 90. This range indicates the relative angle between saw and table. When it is necessary to cut an angle of 10° or one of 125° neither of these figures can be found on the quadrant.

To cut any angle ranging from 0° to 45° subtract the angle to be cut from 90. Set the table or saw for the remainder and use the ripping fence as a guide for the stock being cut. If a 10° angle is to be cut, then 10 from 90 equals 80. The saw is set for this angle and the fence is brought up to the blade.

Angles from 90° to 135° are obtained by subtracting the angle desired from 180° then setting the blade for the remainder. If 125° is the cut wanted, then 125 from 180 equals 55, and that is the angle of the setting. When cuts that come within this angle range are to be cut, the stock is placed flat on the table, and the cutoff guide is used.

Fast Method for Turning Discs on Faceplate of Lathe

THERE are times when many craftsmen have the job of making a number of discs or trays which would normally require a lathe set-up, using a faceplate. The amount of time that would be required to mount each piece on a faceplate would be considerable. This loss of time may be overcome by using a set-up as shown and described here. Sharply pointed screws projecting slightly from the faceplate serve as

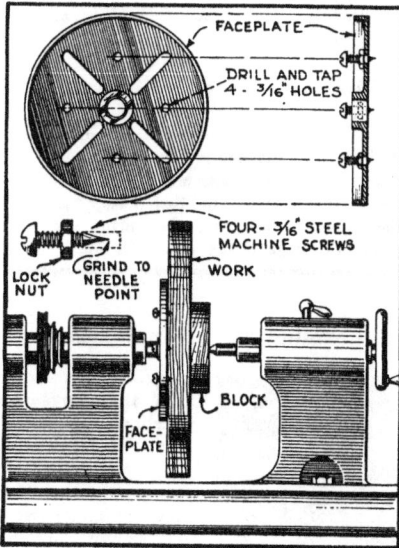

grippers to keep stock from shifting while it is being turned. The set-up is ideal for discs and it may also be used in turning out certain types of trays. To be worked in this manner a tray would be left with a boss in the center, due to the fact that the dead center must be in contact with the work. The currently popular wooden trays for cheese and crackers are of this type.

A regular 6" faceplate may be used by drilling four $\frac{3}{16}$" holes through it. These holes are threaded and fitted with four studs. The studs are made of bolts that have been filed to a sharp point. Each hole should be evenly spaced from the center as well as from each other one. The studs are turned into the faceplate from the back so the points protrude about $\frac{3}{16}$" or $\frac{1}{4}$". The nut locks them in place, but allows adjustment at any time.

To fix the work to the faceplate, the stock to be turned is placed against the faceplate, using the dead center to force pointed studs into the wood. A tray may be turned to within $\frac{1}{4}$" of the bottom without having holes showing as would have been the case if screws were used to hold the work to the faceplate.

The small block between the stock to be turned and the dead center will permit heavier cuts to be made.

• • •

Before starting the motor of a wood-turning lathe, revolve the work by hand to be sure there is sufficient clearance between the wood and the tool rest.

• • •

A few drops of oil on the dead center of a wood-turning lathe will enable the wood to turn more easily and help prevent burning.

• • •

Before you set up a dado head on the circular saw, be sure to brush every speck of sawdust from the arbor. It doesn't take much to make a dado head run out of true—and then it'll vibrate like nobody's business. Also, when placing more than one chipper on the bench-saw arbor between dado blades, arrange the chippers so that they will be at right angles to one another so as to balance well and reduce vibration.

Using Nicked Jointer Knives

IF YOU nick jointer knives by hitting a nail or some other foreign object, you can slide one knife a fraction of an inch to the front edge of the jointer and slide another knife slightly to the rear edge of the jointer, leaving the third knife in the standard position. The jointer then will immediately surface as smoothly as it did originally as the nicks do not come in line. They will no longer nick up the face of the lumber.

When You're Using Power Tools . . .

Blade breakage can be reduced to a minimum on the jig saw by using a blade guide of the proper width and depth. The width of the guide should be just sufficient to allow blade clearance on the side, and the depth should be such as to allow the full depth of the teeth to project beyond the tip.

• • •

Don't forget you can use a small, low-angle block plane to help out in turning straight, slim work. It's not exactly a wood-turning tool, but if it does a clean, accurate job, who cares?

• • •

In adjusting the blade of a band saw, don't try to see how tight you can get it. The blade isn't supposed to be strung like a harp string so that it'll sound a high note when plucked. Either be guided by the tension gauge, if your saw has one, or use just enough tension for the blade to work properly; then if the blade begins to twist while cutting small curves, tighten it a little more.

It's often necessary to jigsaw the end of a molding so that it will fit against another piece of the same molding to make a neatly coped joint. To mark the molding for jigsawing is very easy; in fact, you don't have to mark it with a pencil. Simply make a miter cut on the circular saw or in a miter box, and cut with the jig saw along the line where the miter cut intersects the face of the molding. The end of the molding will then fit perfectly against the mating molding.

• • •

A chipper of the dado head should never be used without a dado saw blade on each side.

• • •

When shaping curved work against a collar, you can see the progress on the cut if the cutter is uppermost. However, if there are variations in the thickness of the stock, by all means mount the collar above the cutter. In that case, too, there's no chance that the cutter will gouge the edge if the work lifts up.

Shellac a Help in Jigsawing

TO GET cleaner cuts when jigsawing designs in plywood, apply a wash coat of very thin white shellac. Liquid shellac purchased in a store added to an equal part of good industrial alcohol will give a consistency thin enough for such purposes. Allow the shellac to dry, which it will do quickly, before sawing.

Guiding Small Jigsaw Work

FOR guiding very small work in a jig saw where the safety fork is in the way and must be raised, use the eraser end of a pencil. With it you can hold down the work firmly yet move it at the same time, thus guiding the work through the saw.

• • •

Rubbing beeswax on a jig-saw blade is a favorite trick of experts who do a lot of fine scrollwork. Try it.

Leveling Power-Tool Stands

HERE is a simple and convenient leveling arrangement for the legs of shop power-tool stands or tables made of angle iron. As shown in the photos, it consists of ¾" bolts and nuts, the nut being welded to the inside of the angle-iron legs.

The same principle can be applied to a machine stand provided with feet as shown in the sketch. A hole slightly larger than ¾", sufficient to allow free passage

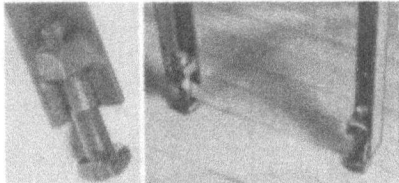

of the bolt through it, is drilled in the foot. The nut is welded to the under surface of the foot.

How to Use a Hollow Chisel Mortiser

THE hollow chisel mortiser is one of the many accessories that may be found in home workshops. This is a tool that is indispensable to the craftsman, as practically any piece of furniture requires the cutting of mortise and tenon joints. There are many points that should be kept in mind when setting up and using the mortiser to insure its satisfactory work and long life. The hollow mortisers that are found on the market today, for the home workshop, may be divided into two groups: those that may be attached to the drill press and those that are units in themselves, usually found mounted on the circular saw stand. In both cases the majority of rules apply but let us consider the mortiser in conjunction with the drill press.

Every drill press has a metal table and as a precaution there should be a piece of wood placed on the table so that if the chisel should slip and drop to the table, the cutting edge will not strike the metal. The chisel itself when placing it in the holder, should have the opening which is found on one of the sides to let out the chips, facing the operator. The type of bit that is used resembles the auger. A regular auger bit cannot be used. The mortise bit is made up in various sizes to fit specific chisels. The bottom is flared out in such a manner so that the hole which it bores will be identical to the outside measurement of the chisel, while the rest of the bit is small enough to fit inside the chisel. When setting the bit in place, be sure that there is enough clearance between the flare of the bit and the edges of the chisel. Should these come in contact with one another, the result will be a ruined chisel or bit and in most cases both are damaged by excess heat caused by fric-

tion. Before turning on the power, the spindle should be turned over by hand to make certain the bit is free of the chisel.

The next item to check, is the depth of the cut. Most drill presses have a scale of some type to show the depth of cut. To set this gauge, place the stock on the piece of wood which covers the table, directly below the bit. The spindle is turned down until the bit comes in contact with the wood. Now, if the gauge is examined, it will show the depth of the spindle at the present time. To this reading on the scale add the amount required for the depth of the mortise and the total amount will be the point at which the stop collar or screw should be set.

The hold down guide is set in place and adjusted to the correct position. Be sure that the chisel clears the fence and prongs of the hold down unit.

When feeding the mortiser into the stock, care must be taken not to force the chisel as it may result in the splitting of this tool. Then, again, be sure the speed of the bit is no more than 500 or 600 R.P.M. While the mortiser is in operation, keep your eye on the opening in the side of the chisel to make certain that the chips are working out. If this is neglected and chips should stick between the walls of the chisel and the bit, excess heat caused by friction will result. Another point to remember is not to make the cut so deep as to bury this opening in the wood as it will prevent the chips from working out.

The chisel and bit should be kept sharp at all times. The former may be sharpened with a small cone-shaped stone, designed especially for such work. The bit may be sharpened in the same manner as any auger bit, with an auger file.

Finger Guard for Key Wrench

MANY home craftsmen know from painful experience that fingers may be caught between the teeth of the key wrench and the chuck of the bench or portable electric drill. To offset such mishaps, drive the handle of the wrench out of its hole, slide a large metal washer up on the key shank to act as a shield, then replace the handle firmly.

Hints on Machine Sanding

WHEN machine sanding, choose a coated abrasive having a grit suitable for the work to be done. For heavy sanding and to remove a great deal of material, use a coarse grit. The finer grits should be used only when finishing.

When sanding on a disk sander, keep the wood in motion so that a large area of the abrasive is used rather than just a small section as would be the case if the material were held in one position. Keeping the wood in motion will help prevent clogging of the spaces between the grits with wood dust.

For roughing—that is, heavy cutting—a medium pressure should be used. If it is found that a heavy pressure is needed to do the work, it means that the coated abrasive has been clogged with dust or the abrasive is too fine for the work.

Finishing requires a light pressure of the material against the drum, belt or disk.

Abrasives that have become clogged should be replaced, otherwise the pressure that will be necessary to do sanding will result in the scorching of the wood.

Machine sanding of wood that contains an excessive amount of resin should be avoided if the coated abrasive is not to be ruined by gumming. Such woods as cypress and pine often contain excessive amounts of resin. These woods if pressed against a coated abrasive will immediately clog the spaces between the grits. If such woods are to be machine sanded, the belt, drum or disk abrasive should be of the type known as "openkote." While such a coat will clog, the abrasive action will last longer than if the grits were applied in a standard coat.

Care of sanding belts pays dividends because they last longer and do better work. There are several products on the market for cleaning sanding belts that have become gummed up and glazed through use. However, a little kerosene applied vigorously with a scrubbing brush will do the work quite satisfactorily. Use the kerosene sparingly to avoid softening the belt. Allow the belt to dry before using it.

The speed with which a belt is run often determines its life. In general, the coarser the belt, the greater the speed at which it may be safely operated. Speeds up to 4,000 feet per minute are not uncommon when a coarse belt is being used.

Certain new types of faceplates designed for power sanding permit the proper grit to be applied quickly. No gluing or cementing is necessary. The changing of the abrasive from a coarse to a fine grit is a simple matter, requiring only a minute.

Dowel Handle for Small Work

FOR holding small articles to be ground and worked on in various ways, such as plastic ear clips or ring settings of plastic, use the lapidary's method of cementing the material to a dowel small enough to permit working completely around. This stem can be used as a handle until the final polishing and then broken off.

● ● ●

When drilling thermoplastics in the drill press, never stop the motor while the drill is in the hole. The cooling of the plastic, if the drill stops, is likely to bind the drill tightly in the hole, or "freeze" it, as the saying goes.

● ● ●

In jigsawing, you can do all kinds of tricks by tilting the table slightly. Many novelties can be made in this way from a single board, because any parts cut at a slight angle can be pushed part way through the parent stock so that they project. For example, you can cut out the letters of your name so that they will appear raised when glued into the opening from which they are cut. And by cutting one part within another, you can make fairly deep articles—even an ornamental box top, lamp base, or ship-model hull.

PART 6
Woods, Plywood and Their Best Uses

WHEN constructing furniture, built-in cabinets or other woodwork in which some or all the members are solid wood (rather than plywood), it is always well to ask yourself, "What effect is shrinkage going to have?"

Few amateur woodworkers realize to what a great extent the humidity in the average house varies from summer to winter. In the winter the air in a well-heated house which doesn't have an exceptionally efficient humidifying system becomes very dry. The relative humidity may be as low as 25 percent in cold weather and 35 percent on normal winter days. In summer, on the other hand, the relative humidity may be 50 or 60 percent.

In this great change from summer to winter, the percentage of moisture in all the wood in the house may vary from about 11 to 6 percent. How much does that represent in shrinkage? A board of Ponderosa pine 1" thick and 5" wide would shrink in width about 1/16". Wider boards would be affected proportionately.

This is why wide panels as shown in Fig. 1 or other members of solid wood should be inserted in frames or otherwise fastened in such a way as shown in Fig. 2 that shrinkage can take place without undue strain either on the board or the joints.

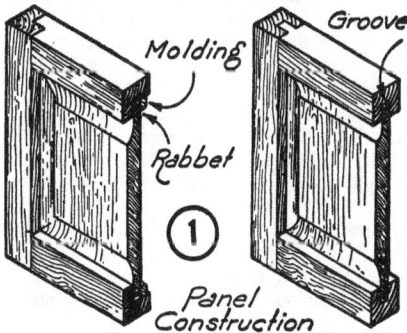

Molding

Groove

Rabbet

①

Panel Construction

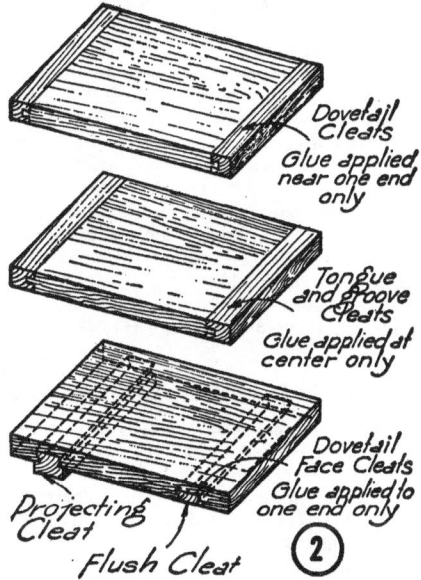

Dovetail Cleats
Glue applied near one end only

Tongue and groove Cleats
Glue applied at center only

Dovetail Face Cleats
Glue applied to one end only

Projecting Cleat

Flush Cleat

②

If a wide panel of solid wood is glued immovably into a strong frame, something will have to give. The panel may work itself loose by breaking the glue joints, but if it can't, the wood itself is likely to crack. For this reason, such panels are allowed to float in grooves or are fastened only along one edge or in the center.

Another common method of allowing wide panels or boards to expand and contract at will is to fasten them as shown in Fig. 3 by means of what is called "slot screwing." In other words, the holes through which the screws pass in the framework or battens are elongated into slots so that the shanks of the screws can slide a trifle as the panel expands and contracts with humidity changes.

In painted paneling, shrinkage may

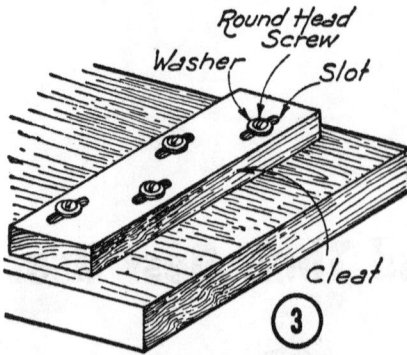

cause unsightly raw lines around each panel. This is sometimes seen in paneled doors which have been installed in a new house and been painted after they have absorbed a certain amount of moisture, as new houses, particularly those with plastered walls, are invariably quite damp. When the house becomes normally dry, the panels shrink away from the stiles and rails and a narrow margin of unpainted wood becomes visible.

The use of plywood for panels and other wide parts avoids shrinkage troubles.

How to Reduce Warpage Troubles

MANY a craftsman has been thoroughly disheartened with the results of warpage after he has completed an otherwise excellent piece of work. There is very little if anything that can be done to permanently correct the damage once it has taken place.

The first point that must be kept in mind is to use nothing but kiln-dried stock for the construction of any piece that is to be used indoors.

If the piece of cabinetwork being made must have a panel that appears to be one piece, then plywood faced with suitable

FIG. 1

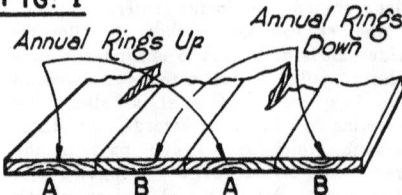

GLUING NARROW STOCK
TO MAKE WIDE PANEL

veneer should be used. If, on the other hand, the piece must be made of solid stock, the wide panel should be ripped into strips 4" to 6" wide, then the pieces arranged edge to edge for gluing together as shown in Fig. 1. Pieces A are arranged so that their annual rings are down while pieces B are placed so that the rings turn upward. These are alternated so that if the pieces should start warping, one will tend to counteract the other.

Another method that is frequently used to control warpage on wide panels is shown in Fig. 2. This consists of a series of saw kerfs cut from end to end. These kerfs may be spaced anywhere from 1" to 2" apart and should be cut quite deep, at least three-quarters of the way through the stock. This particular method for ob-

FIG. 2

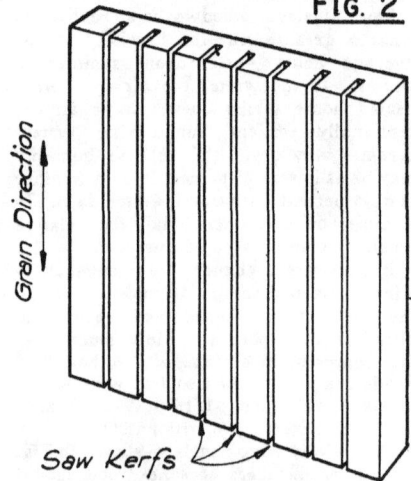

CONTROLLING WARPAGE
OF WIDE PANELS

vious reasons cannot be used as a top member if the ends are to be exposed. It can be used if the saw kerfs are stopped within ½" or ¾" of the ends.

Should a piece of wood warp, there is no way that can be guaranteed to bend the wood back to its original straight surface. It can be straightened temporarily by moistening the cupped side, that is the side that has turned upward. As soon as this moisture has been taken from the wood due to the relatively dry air of the house, the wood will assume its cupped shape.

The only satisfactory way of straightening a warped table top is to plane the surfaces by hand until they are straight. If the panel is badly warped, then it should be ripped into strips about 4″ wide, each piece dressed and jointed individually, and the pieces glued together. With the use of this method, some of the original width will be lost due to ripping, making it necessary to supply another piece of the same stock to achieve the original width.

Plywood Comes in Many Forms

PLYWOOD plays such an important part in all woodworking that most amateur craftsmen take it for granted, just like ordinary lumber.

Fir plywood is the most common type of plywood and serves a great many uses. It is not, nevertheless, a type of plywood to be used for the exposed panels of furniture, for craftwork novelties where appearance is important, for jigsaw work, as a base for laying veneers or plastic veneers, or for any of the better work done by amateur cabinetmakers.

The reason is very simple: Fir is one of the most difficult woods to finish well. It has a coarse grain with alternating hard and soft areas which form a pronounced figure. In common grades of rotary-cut fir plywood, the grain appears about as shown in Fig. 1.

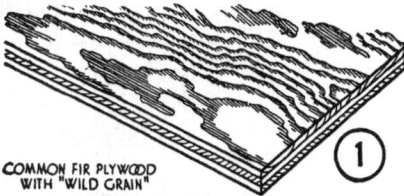

COMMON FIR PLYWOOD WITH "WILD GRAIN"

Since finishing fir plywood is so difficult, why use it when plywood can be obtained faced with so many other woods? If a fine-grain, smooth surface of soft wood is desired, as in much jigsaw work, you can use either poplar, basswood or pine plywood. If a hard, fine-grained surface is needed, maple or birch plywood will serve. If some other cabinet wood is called for, your choice is almost unlimited, because the larger craftwork supply houses and the better-stocked lumberyards can supply plywood in many woods.

In addition, plywood can be obtained with a great variety of Micarta, Formica and other faces, some of which are genuine wood veneer impregnated in such a way as to be cigaretteproof and practically indestructive.

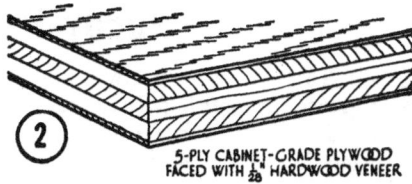

5-PLY CABINET-GRADE PLYWOOD FACED WITH $\frac{1}{28}$″ HARDWOOD VENEER

The most common thicknesses in which plywood is supplied are ¼″, ½″, ¾″ and $\frac{3}{16}$″, but ⅛″ plywood is often available in basswood, mahogany and walnut, and some dealers stock a considerable variety of plywood ⅜″ thick.

You also often have a choice as to whether one or both sides are what is called "good." If the panel is to be seen on both sides, as, for example, when it is to be used to make cabinet doors, it is necessary that both sides be "good."

A further choice is in respect to the number of plies. Plywood ¼″ thick is usually three-ply except when faced with the better cabinet woods, in which case it is often, but not always, five-ply. When thicker than ¼″, plywood of the better grades is made with five plies as is shown in Fig. 2. Even seven plies are not uncommon, but whatever the number, it is always an odd number.

So far we have been discussing what is often referred to as "all-veneer plywood." It is made entirely of sheets of veneer, although these may vary from 1/28″ to ¼″ thick. Much of the better grade of plywood used in cabinet construction is known as "lumber core."

The core of this plywood, as shown in Fig. 3, is made of narrow strips of some relatively stable wood, glued together to form as wide a board as necessary. The core is machined perfectly flat and true.

For cabinetwork, the lumber-core plywood has obvious advantages since it is easier to machine and permits a greater variety of joints to be cut.

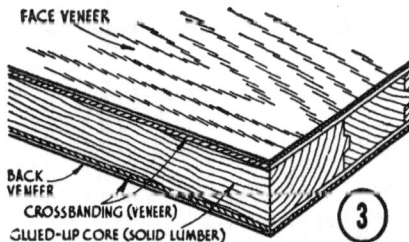

FACE VENEER
BACK VENEER
CROSSBANDING (VENEER)
GLUED-UP CORE (SOLID LUMBER)

LUMBER-CORE PLYWOOD

Ready-Reference Chart of Wood

IN THE chart below you will find at a glance the most important features of the many woods commercially available in the United States.

For comparative purposes, the classifications are described as high, medium and low. Thus a wood marked "H" in shock resistance has excellent re-

WOOD — OTHER NAMES	NATURAL COLOR	TYPE OF GRAIN	GRAIN FIGURE	WEIGHT	HARDNESS	STRENGTH	SHOCK RESISTANCE	ENDWISE COMPRESSION RESISTANCE	RESISTANCE TO DECAY	RESISTANCE TO WARPING
ALDER—Red, Western	Pink to brown	Straight to wavy	Plain or figured	M	M	M	L	L	M	H
ASH—White, Cane, Black, Brown, Green, Hoop, Swamp, Water	White to brown	Straight	Plain or fiddleback	M to H	H	H	H	M	L	M
ASPEN	White to light brown	Straight	Plain	L	L	L	L	L	L	L
BASSWOOD	Cream	Straight	Very mild	L	L	L	L	L	L	L
BEECH—Red-Heart, White-Heart	White to reddish	Wavy, straight	Mild	H	H	M	H	M to H	M	L
BIRCH—Gray, Silver, Swamp, Sweet, Cherry, Black, Mahogany, Yellow	Cream to reddish brown	Straight	Mild	H	H	H	H	L to M	L to M	M
CEDAR—Alaska, Port Orford, Western Red, White	Yellow to reddish brown	Straight	Plain to mild stripe	L	L	L	L	L	H	H
CHERRY—Rum, Wild, Black	Lt red to dk reddish brown	Straight	Mild	M	M	M	H	L	H	H
CHESTNUT	Grayish brown	Straight	Heavy	M	L	M	L	M to H	M to H	H
COTTONWOOD	White	Straight	Very mild	M	M	M	L	L	M	H
CYPRESS	Cream brown	Straight	Mild	M	M	L	M	L	H	M
ELM—American, Slippery, Rock, Hickory, Red, White, Cork, Water, Swamp, Gray	Cream to brown	Straight to Interlocked	Heavy	H	M to H	M	M	M	L	L to M
FIR—Balsam, Douglas, White	White to reddish brown	Straight	Stripe	M	M	M	M to H	M	L	M
GUM, RED*—Sweet, Hazelwood, Satin Walnut	Pink to reddish brown	Interlocked	Slight stripe	M	M	M	M	L	L	L
GUM, TUPELO—Tupelo, Bay Poplar, Cotton, Black Swamp	White to brownish gray	Interlocked	Plain	H	M	L	M	L	L to M	L
HACKBERRY—Sugarberry	Yellow	Straight	Plain	M	M	M	M	L to M	L	M
HEMLOCK—Eastern, Western	Buff	Straight	Plain	H	M	M	M	H	M	M
HICKORY, PECAN—Sweet Pecan, Watery Hickory	Reddish brown	Straight	Faint stripe	M to H	M	H	H	H	L	M
HICKORY, TRUE—Rock, Black, White	White to reddish brown	Straight, wavy, birds-eye	Plain	H	H	M	H	M	L	M to H
LARCH, WESTERN	Reddish brown	Straight	Stripe	H	M to H	M	H	M to H	M	M
LOCUST—Black, Honey	White to yellow brown	Straight	Plain	H	H	H	H	H	M	M
MAGNOLIA—Evergreen, Cucumber	Cream to yellowish brown	Straight	Mild	M to H	L	M	M	L to M	L	H
MAHOGANY—Cuban, Honduras, Mexican, Denin, African, Gaboon, Gambia	Brown to red brown	Straight	Stripe to figure	H	H	H	H	M	M to H	H
MAPLE, HARD—Rock, Black, White	White to reddish brown	Straight, wavy, birds-eye	Varied	H	H	M	H	M	L	H
MAPLE, SOFT—Red, Silver, Water, Swamp, Scarlet, Big Leaf, Oregon, Broad Leaf	White to reddish brown	Straight to wavy	Varied	H	H	M	L to M	L to M	L to M	M
OAK, RED—Black, Red, Spanish, Turkey, Texan, Yellow, Spanish	White to red brown	Straight	Plain to flake	H	H	H	H	H	M to H	H
OAK, WHITE—Burr, Basket, Yellow, Spanish, Chestnut, Cow	Gray brown	Straight	Plain to flake	H	H	H	M	H	M to H	M
PINE, PONDEROSA	White	Straight	Plain	L to M	L	M	M	L to M	L to M	H
PINE, SUGAR	White	Straight	Plain	L	L	L	M	M	M	H
PINE, WHITE	Cream	Straight	Mild	L to M	L	L	M	L	L	H
PINE, YELLOW	Cream to yellowish brown	Straight	Mild	H	M	M	M	L to M	L to M	H
POPLAR, YELLOW	Cream to yellow	Straight	Mild	M	L	L	M	M	L	H
REDWOOD	Cherry to dark mahogany	Straight	Mild	M	L	M	M	M	H	H
SPRUCE, EASTERN—Red, White, Black	White	Straight	None	M	L	M	M	M to H	L	H
SPRUCE, SITKA	Light reddish brown	Straight	Very mild	M	L	M	L to M	M to H	L	L
SYCAMORE	White pink	Interlocked, irregular	Flake	H	H	M	M	M to H	L	L
TUPELO—(See Gum, Tupelo)										
WALNUT, BLACK	Pale br to chocolate brown	Str. to irregular	Varied	H	H	H	M	M to H	H	H

* Commercially Red Gum applies to the heartwood only, while the sapwood is sold as "Sapwood."

Characteristics and Properties

sistance to sudden shock, while one classified as "L" has poor resistance. The columnar headings are self-explanatory. The column headed "Ability to" Take Nails" takes into consideration the holding ability of the wood as well as its resistance to splitting when nails are placed close to the end of a board.

WOOD CONTINUED	RESISTANCE TO SHRINKING, SWELLING	ABILITY TO TAKE NAILS	GLUING PROPERTIES	BENDING	COMPARATIVE EASE OF WORKING				SANDPAPER TO USE FOR BEST RESULTS	PAINT-HOLDING ABILITY	COMMERCIAL USES
					HAND TOOLS	LATHE TURNING	JOINTING, PLANING, SHAPING	SANDING			
ALDER	H	M	M	L	M	M	M	L	4/0	M	Furniture, chairs
ASH	L to M	M	L	M	L	L	M	H	4/0	H	Handles, propellers, bent work
ASPEN	L	M	M	L	H	L	M	M	2/0	M	Pulp, matches, cooperage
BASSWOOD	L	H	H	L	H	L	M	L	3/0	M to H	Boxes, drafting boards, toys
BEECH	L	L	L	M	L	M	M	H	4/0	H	Flooring, chairs, handles
BIRCH	H	M	M	M	L	M	M		4/0	M to H	Dowels, handles, veneer plywood
CEDAR	H	M	M	L	H	L	M	M	4/0	M	Poles, posts, shingles, piling, Venetian blinds
CHERRY	H	M	H	L	L	H	M	H	4/0	L	Furniture, novelties, patterns
CHESTNUT	H	M	H	L	M	H	L	H	3/0	M	Boxes, millwork, poles
COTTONWOOD	L	M	H	L	M	L	L	L	4/0	L	Boxes, crates, toys
CYPRESS	M	H	M	L	M	L	L	L	2/0	M to H	Doors, sash, siding, boats, tanks
ELM	L	H	M	H	L	L	L	M	2/0	M	Cooperage, vehicle parts
FIR	M	M to H	M	L to M	L	L to M	L to M	L to M	5/0	L	Building, siding, timbers, plywood
GUM, RED	L	M	H	L to M	L	H	M	L	4/0	M	Furniture, veneer plywood
GUM, TUPELO	M	M	H	L	M	H	L to M	M	4/0	M	Veneer cores, furniture
HACKBERRY	M	M	M	M	L	L	L	L to M	4/0	M	Baskets, boxes, crates
HEMLOCK	M	H	M	L	M	L	L	M	4/0	M	Framing, sheathing, siding, shiplap
HICKORY, PECAN	L	L	H	M	M	M	M	H	2/0	L	Wheel spokes, ladder rungs, golf-club shafts, dowels
HICKORY, TRUE	L	L	M	M	L to M	M to H	M	H	2/0	L	Wheel spokes, ladder rungs, golf-club shafts, dowels
LARCH, WESTERN	M to H	M	M	M	H	L to M	M	M to H	3/0	L	Rough construction work
LOCUST	H	H	H	M	H	L	M	M to H	3/0	M	Wagon parts, mine timbers
MAGNOLIA	M	M to H	H	L	L to M	H	M	M to H	4/0	M to H	Planing mill products, boxes, Venetian blinds
MAHOGANY	M	M to H	H	L	L	H	M	M to H	4/0	M to H	Furniture, veneer, boat building, fine cabinetwork
MAPLE, HARD	L	L	M	L	L	H	L to M	H	4/0	M to H	Furniture, handles
MAPLE, SOFT	M	L	M	L	L	L to M	L	M	4/0	M to H	Furniture, upholstery frames
OAK, RED	L	M	M	H	L	M	H	H	2/0	M	Used as substitute for white oak
OAK, WHITE	L	M	M	H	L	M	H	H	2/0	M	Ship building, cooperage, flooring, furniture
PINE, PONDOROSA	M	M	H	L	H	M	M	L to M	2/0	H	Core stock for plywood, table tops, low-priced furniture
PINE, SUGAR	M to H	M to H	H	L	H	M	M	L	2/0	H	pattern making, millwork, signs,
PINE, WHITE	M	M to H	L	L	H	L	M	L	2/0	H	boxes, crates, toys, poles, lime
PINE, YELLOW	M	L to M	M	L to M	M	L	M	M	4/0	M	Building construction, boxes, crates
POPLAR, YELLOW	M	M to H	M	M	H	L to M	M	M	2/0	H	Veneer core stock, table tops, low-priced furniture
REDWOOD	H	H	M	M	H	M	L to M	H	3/0	H	House construction, posts, tanks, crates
SPRUCE, EASTERN	M	M to H	H	M	M	M	M	M	3/0	H	Millwork, framing, boxes, crates
SPRUCE, SITKA	M	H	H	L	L	M to H	L	M	3/0	M	Millwork, aircraft construction, baskets, furniture
SYCAMORE	L	H	M to H	L	M	M to H	L	M	3/0	M	Fancy paneling, boxes, millwork
TUPELO	M										(See Gum, Tupelo)
WALNUT, BLACK	M	M to H	H	H	H	M to H	M	H	4/0	M to H	Furniture, veneers, high-grade cabinetwork

Key to Classifications: H = High — M = Medium — L = Low

Index

www.ingramcontent.com/pod-product-compliance
Lightning Source LLC
Chambersburg PA
CBHW031603040426
42452CB00006B/394